£ 10

Postanarch

Saul Newman

———

Postanarchism

polity

The right of Saul Newman to be identified as Author of this Work has been
asserted in accordance with the UK Copyright, Designs and Patents Act 1988.

First published in 2016 by Polity Press

Polity Press
65 Bridge Street
Cambridge CB2 1UR, UK

Polity Press
350 Main Street
Malden, MA 02148, USA

ISBN-13: 978-0-7456-8873-2
ISBN-13: 978-0-7456-8874-9 (pb)

A catalogue record for this book is available from the British Library.

Library of Congress Cataloging-in-Publication Data

Newman, Saul, 1972-
    Postanarchism / Saul Newman.
      pages cm
    Includes bibliographical references and index.
    ISBN 978-0-7456-8873-2 (hardcover : alk. paper) -- ISBN 0-7456-8873-X
(hardcover : alk. paper) -- ISBN 978-0-7456-8874-9 (pbk. : alk. paper) -- ISBN
0-7456-8874-8 (pbk. : alk. paper) 1. Anarchism--Philosophy. 2. Political
science--Philosophy. I. Title.
    HX833.N4976 2015
    335'.83--dc23
                                                        2015012745

Typeset in 11 on 14 pt Sabon by Servis Filmsetting Ltd, Stockport, Cheshire
Printed and bound in the UK by CPI Group (UK) Ltd, Croydon, CR0 4YY

Contents

Preface

What shape does radical politics take today? What sort of imaginary, which political and ethical horizon, animates contemporary struggles? What kinds of alternatives to our current political and economic order are being proposed and fought for?

Asking such questions usually elicits either cynical disdain or sighs of resignation. Everywhere the regime of neoliberal capitalism appears to have prevailed. Even in the wake of its most serious crisis since the Great Depression, when its catastrophic structure was laid bare for all to see, when it seemed to be at its weakest and most vulnerable, global finance capitalism, propped up with massive state support, was resurrected from its apparent demise and now takes on a strange new life. Perhaps this life is an afterlife, but afterlives have an unfortunate tendency to last a long time. Not only has the ongoing economic crisis not brought about the end of neoliberal capitalism, but it has proved merely grist to its mill, allowing, in the form of policies of austerity, even greater incursions of market rationality into everyday life and even more obscene levels of wealth accumulation by a global class of plutocrats. Our lives are increasingly dominated by the dictates of the market, by the imperatives of work, by the spectre of precariousness, poverty and debt. Yet, an inexplicable compulsion to continue as usual grips hold of us, and all the while we are haunted by the ever-present spectre of catastrophe. Alternative horizons seem obscure, almost impossible to imagine. Brief flickerings of resistance appear to have died down or been snuffed out. A great Nothingness engulfs the already exhausted political imagination – an abyss which is in danger of being filled by new and violent forms of reactionary, populist and fascist mobilization.

So where do we look for signs of hope? Despite the apparent bleakness of the current moment, this book does not counsel pessimism or despair. Rather, its aim is to explore the contours of a new kind of political terrain, one that is opened up by the nihilism of the contemporary condition. I want to suggest that, notwithstanding the ambiguous and dangerous ground that we stand on and the seemingly insurmountable nature of the powers we confront, we are nevertheless witness to the emergence of a new paradigm of radical political thought and action, one that takes the form of an autonomous insurrection. Let me be bolder still and say that, if we turn our gaze away from the empty spectacle of sovereign politics, we can glimpse an alternative and dissenting world of political life and action which can only be described as anarchistic. By this I intend to convey the idea of a mode of politics in which self-government and free and spontaneous organization, rather than organization by and through the state, are central.

Autonomous political life

Exemplary of this autonomous form of politics, notwithstanding its relatively short-lived existence and ambiguous and uncertain future, would be the movements of Occupation that have appeared around the world in recent times. The unexpected gathering of ordinary people in squares and public places around the world – from Tahrir Square, to Wall Street, to Gezi Park in Istanbul and the streets of Hong Kong – embodies a wholly new form of political activity, in which the construction of autonomous, self-managed spaces and relations was more important than the presentation of specific demands and agendas to power. While these events took place in different political contexts, they were linked by the common claim of ordinary people to the right to political life in opposition to regimes and systems of power which denied this to them. In doing so, they rejected the usual channels of political communication and representation. The cry of the Indignants in the plazas of Spain was, 'You do not represent us!' This has a double meaning that must be heard and properly understood: it is at once a cry of indignation against a political system that no longer represents the interests of ordinary people and a refusal of representation altogether, a refusal to be spoken for, interpreted (and inevitably betrayed) by politicians. It is as if the denizens of the square were saying, 'You do not represent us and you can *never* represent us!' While this led many, on both the left and the right, to dismiss such movements as anti-political, incoherent and disorganized, such criticisms merely reflected an inability to come to terms with what is an alternative model of radical politics. Moreover, what was genuinely striking about such movements was their rejection of leadership structures and centralized forms of organization. Instead, their originality lay in the networked and rhizomatic forms of political life they engendered.

However, these events, glorious in their audacity, were only the most visible and striking symbols of a broader and more subterranean movement of resistance spreading spontaneously throughout the nerve centres of our contemporary societies. Here, for instance, we could speak of occupations in cyberspace – from WikiLeaks to Anonymous – in which anonymous networks are engaged in a form of information warfare with the state. We could point to mobilizations in support of undocumented migrants and against border policing and surveillance; to autonomous movements of indigenous people; to the dissenting world of climate camps, squats, social centres, alternative economies and ecological communities.

Such spaces, movements and practices, it seems to me, are post-statist. They open up a political terrain which is no longer organized by or directed towards sovereign state power and its representative institutions. The liberal democratic state has suffered a cataclysmic crisis of legitimacy – its veils and garbs have been torn asunder, and the bailout of the banks and the repression of dissent have laid bare the ignominious truth of state

Preface

power and the political elites which govern it. The state in contemporary liberal societies increasingly appears as a sort of empty shell, a vessel without life, a machine of domination and de-politicization which no longer even pretends to govern in the interest of all. Voting in democratic elections and participation in party politics comes increasingly to resemble an arcane religious rite performed by fewer and fewer people. While one may lament political apathy and cynicism, I prefer to speak to a kind of withdrawal from the political form of liberal democracy and the invention of alternative autonomous political spaces and practices, and even the possibility of new forms of political community. It is important to reflect on the way that the autonomous movements referred to above are not directed towards the state – their demands are not addressed to it, nor do they seek to capture state power, in either a democratic or a revolutionary sense. The people who gather in the squares and public places of our metropolises look towards one another rather than towards the state. They embody the desire for autonomous and sustainable life which no longer bears the imprint of the state.

It is for reasons such as these that I believe that anarchism, rather than Marxism or Marxist-Leninism, is the most appropriate prism through which to interpret these new forms of politics. Despite recent attempts, particularly in continental theory, to resuscitate a communist revolutionary form of politics based on rehashed ideas of the party vanguard and a fetishization of the figure of the great revolutionary leader, this Jacobin model, whereby an organized, disciplined revolutionary force seizes the reins of power and uses the coercive apparatus of the state to implement socialism from above, is now defunct. There is no new Robespierre, Lenin or Mao waiting in the wings to lead a revolutionary movement, and the fantasy of seizing control of the state, as though it were a benign instrument to be commanded by a revolutionary will, is no longer plausible, if indeed it ever was. Radical movements today turn their backs on the state rather than seeking to command it, and they reject centralized structures of leadership and party discipline. If there is a horizon of political struggles today – and there is always a danger in positing a single horizon – it is no longer communist, but anarchist or, rather, as I shall go on to argue, postanarchist. This is not to say that the movements and struggles I have referred to consciously identify themselves with anarchism, or indeed with any ideology in particular, but rather to say that their practices, discourses and modes of organization embody an anarchistic ethos in which autonomy and self-organization are the key elements.

Structure of the book

This book develops a political theory of postanarchism. Rather than merely being an updated theory of anarchism, postanarchism is a distinct way of thinking about politics and ethics anarchistically. It draws more on the thought of Stirner, Sorel and La Boétie than it does on Bakunin, Kropotkin and Proudhon. Some of these differences are outlined in the first chapter: the main one being that, while anarchism is a project whose goal is the destruction of state power and the construction of the liberated society, postanarchism emphasizes an anarchism of the here and now, unencumbered by this revolutionary metanarrative. The central idea I introduce here is that of ontological anarchism, derived from Reiner Schürmann and Michel Foucault, which entails a form of thinking and acting without an *arché* – in other words, without stable foundations or essential identities to determine its course.

The next three chapters develop a uniquely postanarchist approach to major areas of contemporary radical politics: respectively, subjectivity, radical action and violence. In chapter 2, I explore the ways in which the governable identities are produced through contemporary neoliberal regimes of power, which, paradoxically, rely on a certain self-subjection. I argue that the only way to escape these mechanisms of control is through autonomous acts of political subjectivation. Yet, I suggest that these can longer be understood in terms of class struggle, identity politics or populist struggles. Instead I propose an alternative political figure here – singularities – an unrepresentable and opaque subject which I theorize through Max Stirner's radical philosophy of egoism. In chapter 3 I suggest that revolution, as a way of thinking about radical political action, is no longer operational, and I propose the notion of insurrection instead. Again drawing upon Stirner's thinking, I understand the insurrection as primarily a form of ethical and political self-transformation in which one distances oneself from power rather than seeking to fight against it directly. I apply this to an understanding of contemporary forms of radical politics which seek to foster autonomous relations and practices outside power, rather than trying to capture it. Chapter 4 explores the problem of violence in radical politics. I argue that, rather than trying to disavow violence, we should transform its meaning. By drawing on the thought of Georges Sorel and Walter Benjamin, I develop the idea of violence as a radical and ethical rupturing of existing social relations which, at the same time, does not shed blood. Here violence is understood as an ontologically anarchic form of autonomous action as pure means without end.

The remaining two chapters are devoted to questions of freedom and autonomy, which are absolutely central to radical politics. However, rather than relying on the familiar normative categories of human emancipation or individual rights – which I argue are largely exhausted today – I approach the question of freedom from the opposite direction, through an encounter with the enigmatic problem of voluntary servitude. So, in chapter 5, I explore Étienne de la Boétie's extraordinary diagnosis of this phenomenon: our strange tendency to will our own domination. However, the implication of this is that all forms of power rely on our self-abrogation, something which reveals to us both the radical potential of the will and the great secret of power – its own non-existence. These implications are explored in the final chapter, in which I outline a postanarchist theory of autonomy, distinct from Kantian and liberal understandings and irreducible to democratic politics. Instead autonomy is based on the condition of ontological anarchy and the realization that we are always and already free.

Postanarchism, in contrast to much of the political theory tradition, is a politics and ethics of indifference to Power. Indeed, I insist on a fundamental distinction between politics and power here. And, rather than seeking to establish new kinds of political institutions or normative foundations, postanarchism affirms the immanent capacity for autonomous life and the ever-present possibility of freedom.

1

From Anarchism to Postanarchism

Anarchism: an outline of a political heresy

If this book is concerned with the theorization of contemporary post-statist forms of radical politics, it is necessary to revisit the political theory of anarchism. Here one immediately stumbles up against a problem: anarchism, more so than other political ideologies and traditions, is difficult to define within clear parameters. It cannot be organized around key names – unlike Marxism and Leninism – although it too has its important theoreticians, some of whom I will discuss in this chapter. Nor can anarchism be confined to a certain periodization, and, although it has had its moments of historical prominence, it has for the most part led the marginal life of a political heresy. Let us think of anarchism, then, as a diverse and heterodox assemblage of ideas, moral sensibilities, practices and historical movements and struggles animated by what I call an anti-authoritarian impulse – that is, a desire to critically interrogate, refuse, transform and overthrow all

1

relations of authority, particularly those centralized within the sovereign state. Perhaps the most radical contention that anarchists make is that the state has no rational or moral justification – that its order is inherently oppressive and violent, and, moreover, that life can function perfectly well without this encumbrance. Anarchist societies are stateless societies, in which social relations are autonomously, directly and cooperatively managed by people themselves, rather than through the mediation of alienating and centralized institutions. It is this implacable hostility to state authority that places anarchism at odds not only with more conservative doctrines but also with liberalism – which sees the state as a necessary evil – with socialism and even with revolutionary Marxism – which sees the state as an instrument, at least in the 'transitional' period, for building socialism, whether through social democratic reforms or through the revolutionary seizure and control of state power.

The debate between anarchism and Marxism is an old one, going back to the nineteenth century when the First International Workingmen's Association was split between the followers of the Russian anarchist Mikhail Bakunin and the followers of Marx, largely over the question of revolutionary strategy and the role of the state. The more 'authoritarian' wing (Bakunin's characterization) of the socialist movement, including Marx, Engels and Lassalle, saw the state as an instrument of class power which, if it was in the hands of the right class – the proletariat led by the Communist Party – could be a useful tool of revolutionary transformation. By contrast, the more libertarian wing regarded the state, *in its essence*, as a structure of domination which would only perpetuate itself after the revolution, rather than wither away as was hoped, and was therefore the main impediment to revolutionary transformation. The state was an apparatus which had therefore to be *destroyed* rather than seized; the pursuit of political power was a trap which would lead only to catastrophe. Other aspects of the dispute involved the organization of the revolutionary party and the question of leadership and authority – which are discussed in Lenin's *State and Revolution* (1918). The implications of this great rift in revolutionary theory and practice have resounded for over a century, being tragically realized in the deterioration of the Bolshevik revolution into the Stalinist totalitarian state. The terms of the Marxism–anarchism debate have been explored elsewhere in great depth, and it is not my intention to go into it here (see Newman 2001). Yet, the most powerful insight that emerges from the anarchist side was that the revolution must be libertarian in means as well as ends, and that, if the means are sacrificed to or simply made to serve the ends, the ends themselves would be sacrificed. This refers to the emphasis anarchists place on 'prefigurative' politics, which is something I shall expand on later.

So anarchism is a form of politics and ethics which takes the value of human freedom and self-government – inextricably linked to equality – as central and sees authoritarian and hierarchical relations – those enshrined not only in the state, but also in capitalism, organized religion, patriarchy, even certain forms of technology – as external limitations and encumbrances upon human freedom. There is a central opposition

3

within the anarchist imaginary between social relations, which, in their 'natural' state, are freely formed and self-regulating, and external structures of power and authority – most prominently the sovereign state – which interfere with these spontaneous social processes and relations, corrupting and distorting them, imprinting upon them artificial, hierarchical and oppressive relations in which human life is alienated. In the words of the eighteenth-century thinker William Godwin, governments 'lay their hand on the spring there is in society, and put a stop to its motion' (1968: 92). The state, this infernal machine of domination and violence, justified neither by religious illusions nor by liberal artifices like the social contract, nor even by modern democratic notions of consent, is the chief obstacle to human freedom and development. As dramatically put by Bakunin, 'the State is like a vast slaughterhouse and an enormous cemetery, where under the shadow and the pretext of this abstraction (the common good) all the best aspirations, all the living forces of a country, are sanctimoniously immolated and interred' (1953: 207).

The end of the metanarrative

We can see how aspects of anarchist thought might resonate strongly with contemporary political struggles, which situate themselves apart from the state and in autonomous relations towards it. When Bakunin, in his revolutionary programme, calls for a different kind of politics – not the seizure of state power in a 'political' revolution but the revolutionary transformation of all social relations (what he calls the 'social revolution') – and when he talks of the need for the masses of the nineteenth century to 'organize their powers apart from and against the state', he seems to be invoking an insurrectionary form of politics in which people autonomously transform their own lives and relations outside the immediate control of the state (see Bakunin 1953: 377). We need to think and rethink what this injunction *'to organize [our] powers apart from and against the state'* might mean today.

However, if the current situation demands a reconsideration of, or even a return to, anarchism, what sort of return is possible here? It seems unlikely that the revolutionary anarchism of the nineteenth century has the same currency today or can even be conceptualized in the same way. The anarchist Alfredo Bonanno (1988), in an honest appraisal of the implications for anarchist politics of the emergence of the post-industrial society in the late 1970s and 1980s, says the following:

> What is dead for them [anarchists today] – and also for me – is the anarchism that thought it could be the organisational point of reference for the next revolution, that saw itself as a structure of synthesis aimed at generating the multiple forms of human activity directed at breaking up the State structures of consensus and repression. What is dead is the static anarchism of the traditional organisations, based on claiming better conditions, and having quantitative goals. The idea that social revolution is something that must necessarily result from our struggles has proved to be unfounded. It might, but then again it might not.

What is being questioned here, I would suggest, is the revolutionary metanarrative that has in the past impelled anarchist thought and politics. Central to this metanarrative is the story of human liberation from a condition of servitude – forced upon an otherwise free and rational being by the corrosive forces of state power – to a condition of freedom and full humanity. In other words, the revolutionary destruction of the State, along with Capital and the Church, and the building of a free society in their place would emancipate man from his situation of oppression, inequality and ignorance and allow him to realize his full humanity. Furthermore, there is at the core of this revolutionary narrative the idea that beneath the layers of 'artificial' political and economic authority there lies a natural commonality, a rational and moral sociability, which is inherent to the human subject but simply lies dormant, latent; this is why anarchism could sustain the idea of social relations as being spontaneously self-regulating once the state was overthrown. Moreover, this innate sociability could be revealed and verified through scientific enquiry. Most famously, Peter Kropotkin (1972) developed his theory of 'mutual aid', as opposed to egoistic competition, which he proposed as an evolutionary and biological instinct that could be observed in both animal and human relations. Murray Bookchin, a modern exponent of this sort of positivist approach – which he terms 'dialectical naturalism' – saw the possibilities of a rationally ordered society embodied within a sort of social totality that is immanent within nature, and whose dialectical unfolding will produce a flowering of human freedom (see Bookchin 1982: 31). Anarchism, as a revolutionary philosophy, has been shaped by the Enlightenment narratives of emancipation, progress and rationalism; it was at once a revolutionary programme and a science of social relations. And it was these narratives which gave it the deterministic quality that Bonanno regards as now defunct. While revolutionary anarchism has never been as deterministic as Marxism – allowing much greater scope for human contingency outside the 'iron laws' of history – it was nevertheless part of a universalizing metanarrative of human freedom, and the social revolution, leading inevitably to the stateless society, was an event that would transform the totality of relations.

This way of thinking about politics and social relations has for some time come into question. Many would claim that we now live in the wake of the crisis of metanarratives; indeed, as Jean-François Lyotard (1991) argued, our late modernity (or postmodernity if one accepts this term) is characterized by a certain scepticism or 'incredulity' towards metanarratives. The universal discourses central to the experience of modernity, the category of a universal objective truth that is or ought to be apparent to everyone, or the idea that the world is becoming more rationally intelligible through advances in science – all these structures of thought and experience have been undergoing a profound process of dissolution due to certain transformations of knowledge in the post-industrial age. Processes of legitimation have become ever more questionable and unstable: the contingency and arbitrariness of knowledge's operation – the fact that it is ultimately based on relations of power and exclusion – is becoming apparent, thus producing a

7

crisis of representation. Moreover, Lyotard pointed to a breakdown of knowledge about society: society could no longer be entirely represented through knowledge – neither as a unified whole nor as a class-divided body. The social bonds which gave a consistency of representation to society are themselves being redefined through the language games that constitute it. There is, according to Lyotard, an '"atomization" of the social into flexible networks of language games' (1991: 17). This does not mean that the social bond is dissolving altogether – merely that there is no longer one dominant, coherent understanding of society but, rather, a plurality of different narratives or perspectives.

Of course, we should not be too sanguine about such developments. Lyotard's report on the 'postmodern condition' was also a report on the emerging *neoliberal* condition, whose logic of 'flexible networks' and atomization it also seems to mirror. However, the decline of the metanarrative refers to a kind of shift or dislocation in the order of social reality, such that we can no longer rely on firm ontological foundations to provide the grounding for thought and, indeed, for political action. Politics can no longer be guided by universally understood Truths or rational and moral discourses, or by a shared experience of Society or Community. Poststructuralist thinkers such as Michel Foucault, Jacques Derrida, Gilles Deleuze and Felix Guattari have engaged in different ways with this dissolution of universal categories. My previous work on postanarchism has emphasized the productive engagement and synthesis between poststructuralist and anarchist theory (see Newman 2001). Chiefly, I showed how the unseating of the universal human Subject from the centre of the order of experience has profound implications for anarchism: subjectivity henceforth had to be seen as constituted through external 'assemblages' of power and discourse, and there can be no clear conceptual separation between the subject who revolts against power and the power which at the same time constitutes his identity and invests him with desire. Foucault's rejection of the 'repressive hypothesis', for instance, and his claim that power was 'productive' – of identities, social relations, truth effects, and even of resistance to it – fundamentally complicates the revolutionary narrative in which the subject liberates himself from the external encumbrances of power. As Foucault famously declared: 'The man described for us, whom we are invited to free, is already in himself the effect of a subjection much more profound than himself' (1991: 30).

From *anarchism to* anarchy

This ontological shift that I am talking about might also be understood in terms of what the Heideggerian philosopher Reiner Schürmann calls the experience of anarchy, which he relates to Heidegger's idea of the closure of metaphysics, a fading away of epochal principles. Unlike in metaphysical thinking, where action has always to be derived from and determined by a first principle, the *arché*, '"anarchy" . . . always designates the withering away of such a rule, the relaxing of its hold' (1987: 6). For Schürmann,

9

> The anarchy that will be at issue here is the name of a history affecting the ground or foundation of action, a history where the bedrock yields and where it becomes obvious that the principle of cohesion, be it authoritarian or 'rational', is no longer anything more than a blank space deprived of legislative, normative, power. (Ibid.)

This gesture of de-grounding, removing or questioning the absolute authority of the *arché* – a form of ontological anti-authoritarianism – is also characteristic of theoretical moves such as deconstruction, which reveals the historicity and discursivity of our accepted structures of thought and experience, thus dislodging the centrality of the figure of Man and what Derrida terms the 'metaphysics of presence'. Schürmann's claim, however, is that this experience of anarchy – understood here as indeterminacy, contingency, event – does not make thinking and action impossible, thereby leading to nihilism.[1] On the contrary, in freeing our experience from the authority of guiding first principles, a certain space is opened up for undetermined free thought and action: questions such as 'what should we do?', 'how should we think?', take on a new and singular urgency as we are confronted with the uncertainty of the ground beneath our feet. The moment of ontological anarchy is thus an experience of freedom and, indeed, intense ethical reflection. Importantly, it also frees action from its *telos*, from the rule of ends, from the strategic rationality which always sought to determine it. Action becomes 'anarchic' – that is to say, groundless and without predetermined ends.

I would like to think about what this experience of anarchy, and specifically the notion of action without the rule of ends, might mean for anarchism. Schürmann is careful to disassociate his conception of anarchy from anarchism: the old masters of anarchism, such as Bakunin, Proudhon and Kropotkin, sought 'to *displace* the origin, to substitute the "rational power", *principium*, for the power of authority, *princeps* – as metaphysical an operation as there has been. They sought to replace one focal point with another' (1987: 6). In other words, the anarchists of the nineteenth century sought to abolish political authority, yet they invoked another kind of authority in its place, the epistemological authority of science and the moral authority of society. Moreover, in place of the state would emerge a more rational form of social organization, the stateless society, of which there have been many proposed visions – collectivist, communal, federalist and, more recently, ecological. However, the anarchy principle would dislodge not only the authority of the current order of the state and political power but also the epistemological authority of alternative, supposedly more moral and rational orders and guiding principles that would replace it.[2]

So does the anarchy principle make anarchist politics impossible? Does it simply turn anarchism into nihilism? Anarchism has always had a slightly ambiguous relationship to the term 'anarchy'. The crude caricature of anarchists as sowers of disorder and chaos – 'anarchy' understood in the commonplace sense – has led anarchists either to distance themselves from this word or to transform its meaning into that of a new kind of order, as expressed in Proudhon's slogan: 'Anarchy is order, government is civil war!' However, if we take

11

the notion of anarchy as simply being 'without *arché*' or without rule or order, then anarchy comes to signify neither disorder nor, as Proudhon intended, spontaneous order, but something rather different. The notion of anarchy that I am developing here, via Schürmann, relates specifically to the idea of thinking and action freed from *telos*, from predetermined ends: '"Anarchy" here does not stand for a programme of action, nor its juxtaposition with a "principle" for dialectical reconciliation' (1987: 6). Is it possible to think of anarchism no longer as a project in pursuit of, and determined by, certain ends – the social revolution that will bring about the stateless society – but rather as a form of autonomous action, a way of acting and thinking *anarchistically* in the here and now, seeking to transform the immediate situation and relationships that one finds oneself in, without necessarily seeing these actions and transformations as leading up to the great Social Revolution, and without measuring their success or failure in these terms? Moreover, seeing anarchism in this way – as a form of action and thought in the present moment rather than a specific revolutionary project – would place less emphasis on achieving the traditional goal of the stateless society. There is no problem with utopian imaginaries, and, indeed, a certain utopian impulse is central to all radical politics in the sense that it punctures the limits of our current reality. However, what guarantees are there that the realization of the stateless society – to the extent that this is a possibility – would not bring with it its own unforeseen coercions? Foucault has taught us to see relations of power as being coextensive with any social formation, stateless or not, which is why he remained sceptical about the idea of revolutionary liberation, arguing that there will always be a need for ongoing modes of resistance and practices of freedom, even in a post-liberation society.[3] I will return to this idea of practices of freedom later.

So, rather than thinking of anarchism as a distinct project, I find it more useful today to see it in terms of a certain mode of thought and action through which relations of domination, in their specificity, are interrogated, contested and, where possible, overturned. What is central for me in anarchism is the idea of autonomous thinking and acting which transforms contemporary social spaces in the present sense, but which is at the same time contingent and indeterminate in the sense of not being subject to predetermined logics and goals. This does not mean that anarchism should not have ethical principles or be impassioned by certain ideals – but, rather, that it should not, and perhaps any longer *cannot*, see itself as a specific programme of revolution and political organization. This does not mean, of course, that all projects should be abandoned, but rather that there is no Project of projects that determines all the others.

Non-power

Perhaps another way to develop this version of anarchism and explore its political implications is through Foucault's idea of 'anarchaeology', a portmanteau word that he uses to describe his methodological approach to the question of the relationship between power, truth and subjectivity. In one of his many studies into the way that we are tied to certain relations of power through our relation to regimes of truth, specifically to the truth about ourselves as subjects, Foucault claims to base his investigations not on a thesis, but on a certain 'standpoint': 'It is an attitude that consists, first, in thinking that no power goes without saying, that no power, of whatever kind, is obvious or inevitable, and that consequently no power warrants being taken for granted' (2014: 77). It is a refusal, in other words, to see power as being grounded in anything other than its own historical contingency – a standpoint that divests power of any claim to universal right, truth, legitimacy or inevitability: 'there is no universal, immediate, and obvious right that can everywhere and always support any kind of relation of power' (ibid.: 78). This is similar to an anarchist sensibility, particularly that of philosophical anarchism, which rejects the idea that we should obey the command of someone in authority *simply because* they are in a position of authority – that, in other words, authority cannot justify itself on its grounds alone. Indeed, Foucault goes on to relate this radical methodological standpoint to anarchism and, at the same time, draws an important distinction: if anarchism – or, as he puts it, anarchy – is defined, firstly, by the claim that all power is bad and, secondly, by the project of the anarchist society in which all power is abolished, his own position, by contrast, does not claim that all power is bad, but simply that no form of power is automatically admissible and inevitable and, furthermore, is not defined by a specific project and end goal. As he puts it:

14

From Anarchism to Postanarchism

It is not a question of having in view, at the end of a project, a society without power relations. It is rather a matter of putting non-power or the non-acceptability of power, not at the end of the enterprise, but rather at the beginning of the work in the form a questioning of all the ways in which power is in actual fact accepted. (Ibid.)

This is a position, Foucault argues, which neither excludes anarchism nor necessarily entails it. Again we have here the idea of an ontological anarchism, in which the emphasis is on anarchy as one's starting point, one's point of departure for political action, rather than being the culmination or the final reward for one's endeavours. So to think about politics anarchistically, which is what I am trying to do in this book, we need perhaps to start with what Foucault calls 'non-power' – a highly suggestive proposition whose implications I shall elaborate later – and proceed from there. Understood in this sense, anarchistic politics today – what I call *postanarchism* – can be understood as starting from the non-acceptability of power, a position which opens up a space of contingency and freedom rather than following a set pattern of anarchism. Postanarchism is anarchism that starts, rather than necessarily ends, with anarchy. This means that it does not have a specific ideological shape and that it may take different forms and follow different courses of action. It might resist and contest specific relations of power at localized points of intensity, on the basis of their illegitimacy and violence; it might work against certain institutions and institutional practices through creating alternative practices and forms of organization. In other words, taking anarchy

15

or non-power as its starting point, postanarchism, as a form of autonomous thinking and acting, can work on multiple fronts, in a variety of different settings, producing reversals and interruptions of existing relations of domination.

2

Singularities

If our radical horizon today is anarchist or, as I have suggested, *postanarchist*, then what kind of political subject populates it? Is there a privileged and identifiable agent of revolution, as could have been said about the proletariat in Marx's time, or has the dissolution of the revolutionary metanarratives which I spoke about in the preceding chapter made the situation today more opaque? In that chapter I laid out the groundwork for a post-foundationalist understanding of anarchism – one that takes ontological anarchy, or what Foucault calls 'non-power', as its point of departure. Just as there is no predetermined revolutionary Project which guides postanarchist ethics and action, so there is no essential identity or universally recognized subject destined for emancipation. The aim of this chapter, then, is to develop an alternative postanarchist conception of subjectivity which evades fixed and representable identities. My claim is that, if we look at contemporary insurrections, we can perceive, amid their flames and intensity, a new mode of political subjectivity which takes *opacity* as its very form of expression. Postanarchist subjects today, in their resistance to regimes of visibility and representation, carve out a terrain of life and a form of existence which is ungovernable to the extent that it is opaque to power. Indeed, the terrain of ontological anarchy which I explored previously suggests to us that the condition of life – insofar as it cannot be said to have any predetermined identity, pattern or *telos* – is in its very essence ungovernable. This does not mean of course that individual lives cannot be subjugated, but that there is always an anarchic dimension to life that exceeds and resists this control. It is these anarchic possibilities of life and their political implications that I am interested in exploring in this chapter. I would like to suggest that, when we come to consider who we are and how we resist today, we should think in terms neither of class – although this is still in other respects important – nor of particularistic identities, nor, worse still, of a People awaiting a Sovereign community – but rather of *singularities*, of self-creating subjects without fixed identity or calling. These singularities, in their very existence – which is becoming increasingly politicized – constitute a form of autonomous life.

The neoliberal government of life

If we are interested in understanding the ways that life today can exceed the grasp of power, we must first consider the ways that power tries to make life governable. All forms of power are premised on a certain capture or subjection of life – or, as I will show in a later chapter, on a certain *self*-subjection. As Foucault has shown us, to be a subject is at the same time to be *subjected*, even if this subjection is never total or irreversible. The operation of power, combined with regimes of knowledge and truth – formations which are historically contingent – has the effect of producing different modes of subjectification, different ways we have of seeing ourselves. And it is through our identification with and attachment to these forms of subjectivity that we are governed, that our behaviour is, as Foucault put it, 'conducted'. Indeed, Foucault's genealogy of modern forms of power reveals a pastoral – or what could be called today a biopolitical – dimension, going back to the ecclesiastical institutions of the early Middle Ages and the idea of the Christian pastorate. This was characterized by the shepherd–flock relationship: the shepherd governs his flock both collectively and individually, each and all, *'omnes et singulatim'* (see Foucault 2000a). This relationship of governing, at the level of both individual subjects and the broader population, finds its expression in the modern state and in liberal or neoliberal rationalities of government: according to Foucault, the disciplinary effects of modern power operate on individual bodies and behaviours, while its biopolitical effects regulate and secure life at the broader level of the population. In this sense, the individual and the modern state form a sort of dyad; modern liberal apparatuses of power do not repress the individual as such but, rather, operate *through* the discursive category of the individual – even through notions of his apparent rights and freedoms – in order to govern him. That is why simply opposing the figure of the individual to that of the state – as perhaps some naïve forms of libertarianism are inclined to do[1] – is problematic and essentially falls back into the very trap of power one seeks to escape. Instead, as Foucault (2000b) proposes:

> The conclusion would be that the political, ethical, social, philosophical problem of our days is not to try to liberate the individual from the state, and from the state's institutions, but to liberate us both from the state and from the type of individualization linked to the state. We have to promote new forms of subjectivity through the refusal of this kind of individuality that has been imposed on us for several centuries.

This implies, he says, a certain kind of anti-authoritarian or 'anarchistic' form of struggle (ibid.: 333). I shall return to this idea later, because, as I shall go on to argue, singularity is not to be confused with *individualism* – at least not in the liberal sense – and indeed implies a rejection of the constrained and over-regulated forms of individuality on offer to us today. Singularity is life in excess of such categories. However, Foucault's general idea of a power that governs or seeks to govern life at its infinitesimal level, by constraining it within representable, statist categories of the individual and the population, with their predetermined capacities and interests, gives us a general framework for understanding the often depleted forms of subjectivity that appear in our contemporary neoliberal societies.

Yet it is probably more precise to say that today the neoliberal societies of control in which we live no longer operate to produce strictly defined categories of individuals – the consumer, the law-abiding citizen, the delinquent, the unemployed, the sexual deviant – but rather bring about a series of affective states and overlapping subjective thresholds, which may traverse the subject in different and contradictory ways. Perhaps we are no longer dealing with the individual, strictly speaking, but with what Gilles Deleuze calls 'dividuals', who are situated within continuous networks of control and productivity (see Deleuze 1992: 3–7). Here power takes the character of overlapping forms of surveillance and regulation rather than of centralized, hierarchical institutions; although these still exist, they are less important than the apparatuses they conceal. In such regimes, the line between the public and private spheres has become indistinct – indeed, has all but collapsed: we have seen, for instance, the almost complete privatization of previously public spaces, institutions and industries, while the private space (the realm of private life, for instance) has become increasingly 'public' – that is to say, *visible* – with ubiquitous surveillance and data-gathering – a condition of hyper-visibility which is actively celebrated and trivialized in reality TV shows. Moreover, the state is increasingly indistinct from corporations and financial institutions in whose interests it so patently acts. Indeed, it is increasingly difficult to discern where exactly sovereignty lies today. Is it within the crumbling edifice of state institutions and functions, or in the governmental elites whose politicians are now expected to lampoon themselves on inane TV game shows? Or does it lie in the anonymous, ever-present form of the Market, whose obscure divinations and pronouncements on a nation's credit rating send governments into paroxysms of fear and embarrassment and which, as Foucault

(2008) claimed, functions today as sovereignty's site of veridiction? Of course, we also see the narrowing of state functions to their policing, securitizing and punitive core; the more the state 'contracts' under neoliberal rationality, the more the institution of the police seems to expand. We are now greeted with the sight of militarized police forces on our streets, increasingly prepared to use lethal violence against unarmed citizens and to harass them for the most trivial of infractions. Given these strange permutations and contortions of the contemporary political space, we need to reflect more carefully on what this means for the subject and for the question of political agency. Certainly, it would seem that the notion of citizenship has all but lost its significance, and struggles for recognition, civic rights and political representation – while still pertinent perhaps to highly marginalized people such as undocumented migrants – take place today on an empty stage.

The neoliberal subject

The neoliberal regime that surrounds us with multiple, overlapping apparatuses of control is totalizing, indeed we could say *totalitarian* – if totalitarianism can be said to coincide today with a certain formlessness. This is an apparatus of power which is difficult to identify or localize in one place, but whose effects, for that very reason, are felt everywhere. Power reaches down into the depths of life in an unprecedented way: the whole of life is measured, regulated and judged by the axioms of the market, and if the biopolitical state appears not all that interested any more in securing the conditions of life (power today no longer seems to care that much whether we live or die),[2] this simply highlights the degree to which market logic has permeated governmental rationality. Yet, to the extent that we remain alive, we are inserted into an apparatus which seeks to capture every facet of existence and desire within its circuits – of consumption, communication, spectacle, hyper-visibility, idiotic enjoyment, endless and meaningless work, debt and constant insecurity – creating an unlimited dependency. However, this state of dependency and control is a curious thing because it takes the formal shape of freedom and independence. The totalizing nature of the neoliberal regime lies in the fact that we are governed in the name of our own freedom (we are expected to be free, self-reliant rational choosers); the subject is thrust back upon himself and his own resources, making his life one of constant uncertainty, which allows him to be more effectively governed. Spaces are provided for individual differences and tastes, but only through their commodification, thus producing unparalleled conformity. This regime no longer cares what we think – we are granted a certain freedom of thought – as long as we obey through our everyday practices, behaviours and rituals. As I shall go on to show in a later chapter, it is only through the *continuity* of these behaviours and rituals, in which our desire is constantly invested, that neoliberal power is sustained. The Master we obey is an invisible one, and in many ways only a creation of our own obedience, yet we nonetheless obey it as though it were absolute. It is not true, moreover, that neoliberal capitalism obliterates all social bonds; rather it creates new and tighter bonds, which we renew every day, that compress us ever closer into a spectral social body.

We can identify a number of subjective states produced by this strange machine, affective intensities that overlap with one another in the contemporary (in) dividual. For instance, we are subjected to ubiquitous apparatuses and measures of security, from the most mundane and everyday (surveillance cameras, data-gathering through internet searches, and so on) to the most terroristic – draconian anti-terrorist and border-control measures and exceptional police powers. We live in regimes of hyper-visibility in which everything must be on display and where we must continually offer ourselves up for inspection. One only has to observe passengers passing through airport security, who make such a show of their compliance, who want to appear *only too happy* to have their bodies scanned and luggage searched. Yet, if our lives must be continually secured, why do we feel so insecure? Why do enhanced security measures only make us feel more anxious? Because we start to fear security more than the thing we are being secured against; we dread the day when we might come to the attention of the authorities, when we come to appear, even mistakenly, as a subject of risk, a suspicious individual.

Of course, what contributes to our anxiety – and we should note the fact that anxiety, along with other mental disorders, is becoming more prevalent today – is the situation of economic precariousness that most of us find ourselves in; haunted by the spectre of unemployment, debt and poverty, we cling on to what we have, terrified of losing our jobs, of sinking into financial oblivion. Therefore we work longer and harder than ever, and, with modern communications technology, we are always at work, always contactable, always willing to do whatever is asked of us. So the precarious subject is also a docile and obedient subject; the spectre of economic destitution, of descending into 'bare life', as well as the threat of an increasingly punitive state, works to keep us in line. Yet there is something more, a kind of *voluntary servitude* that is more difficult to account for and which I shall go on to explore in a later chapter.

Obedience and docility are also induced today through everyday habits of consumption and communication. The contemporary subject is a constantly *distracted* subject. Much has been written about the jarring, disorienting effects of the superfluous information and images we are overloaded with today, and the cognitive dissonance and subjective unhappiness produced by our total immersion into the circuits of communicative capitalism. We suffer from a kind of technology-induced attention deficit disorder. Not only are we over-stimulated by constant semiotic activation through intrusive and all-pervasive communicative technologies, beyond the limits of what our organism can bear (see Berardi 2009), but we are also lured, through participation in social media and blogging, into circuits of capitalistic *jouissance* accompanied by networks of surveillance (see Dean 2010). While there is no doubt that these communication technologies also provide powerful tools of anonymity and resistance, there is a danger here of their fetishization. The abundance of information is at the same time somehow disabling:

we know what is going on – the secrets of state and corporate power are revealed and documented in all their obscenity – and yet we often feel powerless to act, beyond the impotent gesture of 'clicktivism'. While the unmasking of power through communication is unquestionably a good thing, simply making it transparent is not enough. Indeed, one gets the sense that today it no longer matters whether power is naked or clothed, as long as one continues to obey. Moreover, there is little to support the claim made by some of the giddy enthusiasts of such technologies, of a new revolutionary class of the cognitariat emerging through the networks of communicative capitalism, as the proletariat was thought to do in Marx's time.[3] The radical potential of these technologies is much more ambiguous, as are the forms of subjectivation they produce. What seems clear is that the answer to the deadlock in which radical politics finds itself today does not necessarily lie in more or better communication. Deleuze, in a conversation with Toni Negri, puts it well:

> You ask whether control or communication societies will lead to forms of resistance that might open the way for a communism understood as the 'transversal organization of free individuals.' Maybe, I don't know. But it would be nothing to do with minorities speaking out. Maybe speech and communication have been corrupted. They're thoroughly permeated by money – and not by accident but by their very nature. We've got to hijack speech. Creating has always been something different from communicating. The key thing is to create vacuoles of noncommunication, circuit breakers so we can elude control. (Deleuze and Negri 1995)

What can be taken from this suggestive claim is that the coming politics will not be about communicating the demands of representable identities seeking visibility on the public stage. Politics will not be about struggles of recognition, nor will it be based on the idea of rational communication. Rather, it will take the form of *incommunicability* – that is, opacity and anonymity. I will return to this point later.

What contributes further to our distracted and enervated condition is not only the religion of consumerism – whose capturing of our desires still constitutes the biggest hurdle to any sort of radical transformation – but also the simulated world of mediatic spectacles, in which politics itself is reduced to the banality of a game show, and in which mega events like the Olympic Games and the World Cup seem to serve the same function in neoliberal regimes as 'bread and circuses' did in ancient Rome. The insurrections against the ignominious spectacle of the World Cup in Brazil in 2014, amid the poverty of the favelas, are a hopeful signal that the magical power of the spectacle in our societies is starting to dissolve. Overcoming consumerist desire, which is so deeply embedded within our subjectivity, is a much bigger obstacle – requiring as it does new forms of subjectivation, and maybe even an affirmation of a certain kind of 'austere life' – a life which consumes only what is absolutely necessary.

Yet, radical politics must at the present moment confront the increasingly pathological, reactionary and psychotic forms of subjectivity appearing on our horizon. Idiocy, and a general emptying out of meaning, can be encountered everywhere, from our fascination with the most mind-numbing TV shows and banal forms of entertainment to the absolute trivialization of political discourse and a general cultural infantilization. And the impotence of our lives also seems to encourage not the rejection of the current order, which renders us as such, but rather a seething resentment against certain marginalized groups – the poor, immigrants – which comes out in increasingly xenophobic and racist, even fascistic forms of politics. The uncanny return of all kinds of fundamentalism, as a nihilistic reaction to the condition of ontological anarchy, threatens to inflict untold violence on the world. Depressive and suicidal impulses are another symptom of the alienated world in which we find ourselves, a normal response perhaps to an abnormal situation. Such are the dangerous, destructive and self-destructive pathologies that we recognize all around us and sometimes within ourselves, and which any honest assessment of the possibilities of radical politics today must contend with.

Radical subjects

Despite this rather gloomy picture, we see many hopeful signs of resistance. The regime of control that I have diagnosed, while totalizing in its logic, does not always work. There are flickerings all around us of insurrection, offering us a glimpse of alternative modes of political subjectivation characterized by a desire for autonomous life. I have discussed forms of political mobilization associated with the Occupy movement but have also pointed to more everyday subterranean and rhizomatic forms of resistance and direct action, such as can be found in hacking computer networks. My claim is that these practices embody a new form of subjectivity and action which cannot be adequately captured within the more familiar categories of politics. Rather, what distinguishes contemporary radical subjectivities is the refusal of any kind of representable identity. Indeed, we could say that they embody a gesture of *dis-identification*.

Contemporary radical struggles are struggles against the capitalist way of life and against a state-backed financial system that has plundered people's livelihoods across the globe; economic concerns form the backdrop of many struggles today, and they emerge out of work, its miseries, its insecurity, or the sheer lack of it. Moreover, with the intensification of processes of neoliberal capitalism throughout the world, with its rapine exploitation of human beings and the natural world, with its unequal distribution of wealth and resources, we could speak of a general process of enclosure and subjugation, which is perhaps experienced differently in different contexts, but whose general logic is essentially the same everywhere. Yet, at the same time, it is clear that, in our post-industrial societies, the Marxian understanding of the proletariat as the universal revolutionary class, organized and led by the Communist Party, is no longer valid. Even in Marx's time, anarchists pointed to what they saw as the narrow and exclusivist nature of a revolutionary politics organized around the industrial working class as the privileged subject; they preferred instead the notion of 'mass', which was more heterogeneous and would include the peasantry and lumpenproletariat (see Bakunin 1950:

47). Today, although a class dimension is still present in many struggles, it is no longer possible to think in terms of a proletarian class consciousness or a unified working-class movement. Subjectivities today are simply too dispersed, fragmented and heterogeneous for this; the metanarrative of the great proletarian revolution has collapsed, and the labour movement – at least in most Western societies – has, since the post-war years of the last century, been diverted into now ossified social democratic political parties and trade unions.

Equally inadequate, if not more so, would be to see contemporary struggles through the lens of 'identity politics' – that is, struggles for recognition and rights on behalf of particular marginalized identities. With some possible exceptions – such as the rights claims of certain religious and ethnic minorities living under theocratic and authoritarian regimes, or those of indigenous people, or the struggles of undocumented migrants in liberal societies – nothing could be less challenging to the neoliberal order than the desire for recognition on the part of particular identities, whether cultural, sexual or otherwise. Such claims for political and cultural recognition, while important in the past, are now simply inscribed within the neoliberal state order, incorporated through its logic of representation in which differences and particularities, so long as they are identifiable and representable, are simply accommodated by existing institutions: even many conservatives these days support the idea of gay marriage, for instance. Identity politics risks falling into an essentialist trap where one is in a sense imprisoned within one's own subjectivity, whose interests and desires have been carved out for it by power; it is well to recall Foucault's insight that the task of politics today was to not discover who we are 'but to refuse who we are' (2000b: 336). Moreover, the assertion of a particular marginalized identity often produces forms of *ressentiment* based on a perception of one's own suffering and victimization, or what Wendy Brown (1995) calls 'wounded attachments'. There is a kind of narcissism at work in certain forms of identity politics, in which the insistence on one's discrimination at the hands of sexist or heteronormative institutions comes to be the thing that defines one's identity. At best, identity politics becomes a benign form of liberalism, obsessed with the representation of ever more particular and marginal identities – as in L-G-B-T-Q. At worst, in the insistence of an authentic identity that is constantly victimized, identity politics becomes akin to a form of fundamentalism. Either way, this kind of politics of representation and recognition has reached a point of exhaustion.

Can contemporary struggles be said, on the other hand, to be populist? Are they enshrined in a new figure of the People? While there was perhaps a faint trace of populism in Occupy's slogan of the 99 per cent – albeit highly symbolic and abstract – radical struggles for autonomy cannot be encapsulated within the logic of populism. And while some radical thinkers such as Ernesto Laclau (2005) and Jodi Dean (2012) have, in different ways, sought to theorize new forms of populist struggle, the problem with this approach is that it inevitably invokes a sovereign politics, whereby the figure of the People exists only insofar as there is a Leader who represents them. The People is ultimately always the figure of the state. We recall the fearsome frontispiece of Hobbes's *Leviathan*, which depicts the People as a unified, totalized figure compressed within the body of state; the individuals who make up this collective 'body politique' gaze up with eyes of fear and love towards their sovereign Master. Today the People is an increasingly archaic figure for politics, hinged as it is to the crumbling nation-state order, whose decomposition seems only to incite nationalism and racism. While not all populisms are racist – indeed they are in some contexts socially progressive and emancipatory – nationalism and racism remain their permanent temptation.

The politics of the incommunicable

In contrast to these previous categories, all of which are based on a certain representable political subject, contemporary postanarchist subjectivities take on an entirely different shape – that of the refusal of representation altogether. As I have already noted, what is often characteristic of many forms of radical politics is the refusal not only of formal modes of political representation – political parties, participation in elections, and so on – but also of the communication of political demands. The aim is not to communicate demands and proposals to Power, because this only affirms the position of Power; it is not to be a counter-Power or counter-hegemony. Rather it is to generate forms of autonomous political interaction and intensity. This perhaps explains the importance of non-verbal, gestural language found in many forms of activism today

– whether signals of agreement or dissent in collective decision-making in the Occupy camps, or the ironic and moving gesture of holding up one's hands (to say 'Don't shoot!') in condemnation of recent police violence in the United States, or the spontaneous mass gatherings of people that we now see in public spaces (what used to be called 'flash mobbing' but which has now taken on a greater political resonance). This politics of gesture should be placed alongside other forms of direct action which have been going for quite some time – such as destroying GMO crop fields and disrupting global capitalist summits.

One gesture is particularly striking and significant, and that is the covering of faces and the concealing of identities in mass gatherings. For years participants in the anarchist black bloc covered their faces with ski-masks and bandanas before engaging in direct confrontations with police in anti-capitalist demonstrations.[4] Now, the wearing of masks – particularly the ubiquitous 'V' mask, which has become a universal symbol for Anonymous – is a commonplace feature of activist convergences in many parts of the world. What is the significance of the wearing of masks? This has to be seen as more than just a practical counter-surveillance measure, although it is this as well; we know that at any demonstration or gathering today, even the most harmless, there are hordes of police photographing protestors. More significantly, it is a symbolic gesture of invisibility and anonymity – in other words, a refusal to be made visible and therefore to be made representable within a particular identity. In our regimes of hyper-visibility, which demand that everything is on display and that everyone confirm their identities, maybe the most radical gesture is to disappear, to become anonymous, imperceptible. Invisibility becomes a kind of weapon. The Invisible Committee's insurrectionary handbook, *The Coming Insurrection*, counsels us to '*Flee visibility. Turn anonymity into an offensive position*' (2009: 112; emphasis in original). And yet this refusal of visibility becomes at the same time a highly visible political gesture – it makes subjects *appear* in all their intensity. We can perceive here, moreover, a symbolic rejection of the whole logic of recognition and therefore of identity politics – identities and differences become imperceptible in this anonymous mass of masks. The Invisible Committee goes on to say: 'To be socially nothing is not a humiliating condition, the source of some tragic lack of recognition – from whom do we seek recognition? – but is on the contrary the condition for maximum freedom of action' (ibid.: 113). Yet, as I shall show later, this interaction with an anonymous body means not the eclipse of the subject within a collective organization, such that his or her differences are negated, but rather a completely different form of political relation which may be termed *singularities*.

Also striking here is the appearance of Anonymous as a paradoxical symbol of contemporary activism – not so much a group, and certainly not a formal political organization, but rather a rhizomatic formation of anonymous individuals that spreads through the networks of our neoliberal control societies, disrupting its circuits at critical points, hacking into government databases, revealing corporate and state secrets, eavesdropping on the eavesdroppers and wreaking as much havoc as possible within the system of power – creating, as Deleuze put it earlier, 'vacuoles of noncommunication'. The fact that government agencies simply do not know how to deal with this assault on their apparatuses of control and surveillance is indicative of the power and resonance of invisibility today. Foucault once said that he wrote in order to have no face. Perhaps, in the same way, singularities today make themselves invisible, efface and dis-identify themselves, in order to create a space for autonomy and freedom of political action.

Singularities

So how should we understand this notion of singularity – a form of subjectivity which eschews strictly defined identities and creates for itself, in association with others, an autonomous space of existence? There have been a number of approaches to this in continental philosophy. Giorgio Agamben, for instance, has developed the notion of singularities – what he calls *whatever singularity* – as a new kind of post-sovereign figure which cannot be assimilated within the representative structures of the state and whose appearance in spontaneous political gatherings suggests the possibility of an entirely new post-identity form of politics. 'Whatever singularities' form a 'coming community' which is identified not through any particular category but simply by the condition of belonging – a sort of open, amorphous community without identity and borders. Insofar as this community of singularities eschews representation within predetermined categories (national, religious,

class), it presents, according to Agamben, an unaccepta-
ble threat to the state, whose only response is to declare
war on it. In a haunting and in some ways prescient
passage, which invokes an anarchistic political horizon,
Agamben says:

> *The novelty of the coming politics is that it will no
> longer be a struggle for the conquest or control of the
> State, but a struggle between the State and the non-State
> (humanity), an insurmountable disjunction between
> whatever singularity and the State organization.* (1993:
> 54.5; emphasis in original)

Yet, he goes on to say that this insurrection of singularities against the state is not the same as the simple
opposition between society, or the social principle, and
the state – a binary, Manichean opposition which, as I
suggested, characterized the revolutionary anarchism of
the nineteenth century. Rather, 'whatever singularities'
cannot form a society or social body because they do not
affirm any sort of identity. This is an important qualifi-
cation, which, as I will argue in the following chapter,
allows us to make a distinction between revolution and
insurrection. The key point here is that postanarchism
does not anchor itself in the idea of a coherent social
body, based on pre-existing forms of community life
and relations of sociality, but, rather, presupposes an
undoing or rupturing of this body. Agamben's notion of
'whatever singularity' is related to his deeper interest in
what he calls form-of-life, by which he means 'a life that
can never be separated from its form, a life in which it
is never possible to isolate something like a naked life'
(2000: 3). Politics in the Western tradition has, since

antiquity, been based on the separation of biological or bare life (*zoé*) from politically qualified life (*bios*). While in the modern biopolitical era we have seen the eclipse of this distinction, such that biological existence becomes the very object of political calculations and rationalities – producing bare life as captured in the sovereign state of exception – Agamben's claim is that this development at the same time opens up new possibilities for an alternative politics of life. This would involve a certain understanding of subjectivity in which the way one lives one's life always embodies an ever-present political potentiality. This new political subject has, as I would see it, an ontologically anarchic existence in the sense that it is no longer defined by biological essence, vocation, project or destiny. It points to the importance of reclaiming the possibilities of an autonomous and contingent political life for its own sake.

Agamben's understanding of singularity suggests the possibility of a new form of association with others, which is defined not by a specific identity but simply by belonging. Indeed, one of the central tasks of political theory, it seems to me, is to rethink the very idea of community in ways which, on the one hand, no longer construct absolute borders and exclude and, on the other, no longer assimilate and crush those who are included. I shall say more about this later, but another thinker who has approached this question, once again through the notion of singularity, is Jean-Luc Nancy. In the era of the dissolution of the notion of community – symptomatic of the breakdown of metanarratives and the eclipse of universal horizons that I spoke about in chapter 1 – Nancy argues that it is no longer possible to restore the idea of an organic, immanent community, defined by an essence; this can lead only to totalitarianism. Instead, he proposes the idea of a community of non-essence, non-immanence, defined not by any particular identity but by its own openness and finitude. Nor should community be defined by a specific *telos*, work of production or project to be achieved – such as achieving the destiny of Humanity or Freedom or, in the case of anarchism, the stateless society; as I showed in chapter 1, the anarchism of the revolutionary project of freedom gives way to a postanarchism that instead takes ontological freedom as the *starting point* for any understanding of politics and community. At the same time, for Nancy, the answer does not lie in the figure of the individual, as distinct from community; the individual – at least in the liberal sense – is a symmetrical figure to that of the absolute community, insofar as it is a self-enclosed sovereign totality (1991: 3). Nancy's claim is that this atomism of the individual subject is impossible because the very notion implies relations with others insofar as one differentiates oneself from others, and therefore there is an inevitable opening out onto the world. Community, then, should be thought of simply in terms of a relation of openness which undoes autarchic, sovereign identities and makes impossible closure and totality of any kind.

It is here that one encounters the idea of singularity – and a community of singularities – as distinct from the atomized individual and in opposition to the notion of the absolute. For Nancy, singularity is a kind of finitude, a relational space of sharing with others – what he calls elsewhere *being singular plural* (see

Nancy 2000: 1–99) – which foregrounds Being,
essence is therefore finite; indeed singularity, insc
it disrupts the consistency and sovereignty of an,
tity by in a sense de-grounding it, is linked to the idea
of ontological anarchy developed earlier. Community
can be seen as the coexistence or co-appearance (what
Nancy calls *compearance*) of these singularities, whose
being-in-common is not grounded on any prior social
being or identity but is always contingently defined by
those singularities themselves: 'there is no communion
of singularities in a totality superior to them and immanent to their common being' (Nancy 1991: 28). So his
notion of an 'inoperative community' of singularities is
by necessity an open community, without essence, identity, borders or predetermined project, an ontologically
anarchic community which is always 'unworking' itself
and opening itself to that which is beyond it.

The unique one

Nancy understands singularity as a form of uniqueness
or plurality which is irreducible to abstractions and
determined identities – such as Man, Humanity, Society
(which always risk doing a violence to singularity, swal-
lowing it up into a totality) – but which at the same time
is unique only insofar as it coexists or co-appears with
others. It is here that I want to develop the notion of singularity and the possible forms of coexistence it fosters
through a different, yet in some ways intersecting, route
– that of the egoistic philosophy of the little-known
nineteenth-century philosopher Max Stirner. Stirner's

radically anti-essentialist anarchism – if indeed it can be called that – is, as I have suggested elsewhere, a key point of reference for postanarchist political theory (see Newman 2011). While it might seem paradoxical that I am drawing on a thinker who tends to be regarded as an exponent of an extreme form of individualism, I want to suggest that his notion of the ego – *der Einzige*, which is more accurately translated as 'the unique' – cannot be reduced to anything like a liberal individualism, or indeed to any identity at all, and is better understood in terms of singularity. Indeed, Stirner gives us a clearer and more substantive notion of singularity than Agamben and Nancy, one that is much more useful for understanding contemporary postanarchist subjectivity.

In his only major work, *Der Einzige und sein Eigenthum* (commonly translated as *The Ego and its Own*,[5] although more accurately so as 'The Unique and his Property'), published in 1845, Stirner, the most radical member of the Young Hegelian circle, launched a devastating assault on the philosophical tradition – in particular, Hegelian thought – as well as the humanism of his contemporary Ludwig Feuerbach. Stirner may be justly regarded as the first theorist of the decline of meta-narratives, the one who, even before Nietzsche, peered behind the visage of Man and saw God reinvented. Thus, according to Stirner, the humanist rationalist project, associated with Feuerbach, of replacing God with Man merely reaffirmed the category of Divine by making Man himself into a sacred being and the supposedly secular categories of rational truth, morality, and so on, into theological precepts. Stirner exposes humanism, and its political discourses of liberalism

and socialism, as simply part of a chain of substitutions
through which the abstract and alienating category of
the sacred is rearticulated in secular garb. Therefore,
for Stirner, 'The human *religion* is only the last meta-
morphosis of the Christian religion' (1995: 158).[6] So
the figure of Man, according to Stirner, imposes upon
the subject a new kind of alienation insofar as he is
now expected to live up to certain universal standards
of rationality and morality and to search within himself
for a sacred 'human essence'. As Stirner declares, then,
'"Man" is the God of today, and fear of man has taken
the place of the old fear of God' (ibid.: 165).

For Stirner, then, we live in a haunted world, a world
of abstractions, apparitions, or what he calls 'spooks':
'Man, your head is haunted ... You imagine great
things, and depict to yourself a whole world of gods
that has an existence for you, a spirit-realm to which
you suppose yourself to be called, an ideal that beckons
to you' (1995: 43). We are enthralled to what he calls
'fixed ideas' – such as human essence, morality, rational
truth, society, freedom – which are claimed to be universally understood and to which we must aspire. Yet,
these are simply religious abstractions, illusions without
any basis in reality. As an exponent of ontological anarchy, Stirner shows that there is no essential truth at the
base of our world, no firm foundations upon which we
must live our lives; there is only an abyss of nothingness,
which means that it is up to the individual – or what
he prefers to call the egoist or 'owner' – to determine
for himself his own life. As Stirner says, 'the essence of
the world, is for him who looks to the bottom of it –
emptiness' (ibid.: 40).

Stirner's anti-essentialism means that the subject cannot be assimilated into the fixed, determined identities that have been established for him: 'I am neither God nor *man*, neither the supreme essence nor my essence, and therefore it is all one in the main whether I think of the essence as in me or outside me' (1995: 34). Yet, it is the attempt to subjectify individuals within these categories that creates as a by-product certain forms of degraded or deviant subjectivity, what Stirner refers to as the UnMan (ibid.: 159), or what Agamben might call 'bare life'. We can see here how this critique of essentialism and humanism resonates with poststructuralist approaches to the subject, and particularly with Foucault's invitation to 'refuse who we are', as a form of resistance to the liberal 'government of individualization'. Indeed, Stirner considered the ways in which liberal political regimes constructed certain figures of the individual as bearers of rights, who were supposedly free, or needed to be freed, and yet who, through these very fictions, were tied ever more firmly to the state: 'It does not mean my liberty, but the liberty of a power that rules and subjugates me' (ibid.: 96). In other words, the freer the individual according to the coordinates of liberal ideology, the freer the state was to govern the individual. For instance, the notion of formal equality of rights does not recognize individual difference and singularity but, rather, swallows it up into an imaginary totality – the body politic or state. There is nothing wrong with equality as such, for Stirner; it is just that, in its embodiment in the liberal state, the individual is reduced to a fictional commonality which takes an institutionalized form. The 'equality of rights' means

42

only that 'the state has no regard for my person, that to it I, like every other, am only a man' (ibid.: 93). Rights are granted, through the state, to Man – to this abstract spectre – rather than to a real person. Indeed, Stirner sees liberalism not so much as a particular regime but rather as a kind of subjectifying machine which takes different forms – *political, social* and *humane* – through which the progressive liberation of Man is concomitant with the elimination of the ego.

So what kind of existence might the subject have beyond this world of abstractions, spooks and political and social institutions which seek to turn him into Man? For Stirner, the position we must adopt is to affirm the ego as our only concrete reality and take this as our starting point as we encounter the world. As Stirner declares, 'Nothing is more to me than myself!' (1995: 7). It is this position which has prompted certain misinterpretations of Stirner – as a solipsist who denies the existence of external reality or as a proponent of selfish individualism. Rather, in taking the ego as the only ontological reality, he is seeking to undermine the authority of transcendental concepts and their hold over us and inviting people to affirm themselves, in their uniqueness and singularity, as their only cause. Stirner's philosophy of egoism is a programme of autonomy, or what he calls 'ownness', which I shall discuss in greater detail in later chapters. Yet, as I have said, egoism is not to be conflated with individualism, which is a liberal subjective category. Rather, it should be understood in terms of singularity and uniqueness. Moreover, and this is the important point, this singular ego is not an essence of any kind – it is not an individual with a set of properties and interests; rather, it is a kind of *nothingness*, what Stirner calls a 'creative nothing', in a constant state of flux and becoming, consuming itself and creating itself anew. The subject as singularity is one of absolute uniqueness – not only, or not even, in the sense of difference, which can be quite a limited aspiration, but in the sense of being *indefinable*:

> They say of God, 'names name thee not'. That holds good of me: no *concept* expresses me, nothing that is designated as my essence exhausts me; they are only names. Likewise they say of God that he is perfect and has no calling to strive after perfection. That too holds good of me alone. I am *owner* of my might, and I am so when I know myself as *unique*. In the *unique one* the owner himself returns into his creative nothing, of which he is born. (Ibid.: 324)

To be singular is to be *undefinable*, and, as I have suggested above, to be undefinable, or unrepresentable, is to be *ungovernable*. We find a strong parallel here with Agamben's notion of 'whatever singularity', and indeed with contemporary political experiments in anonymity.

The union of egoists

Yet, what kind of community is possible among these singularities? Stirner rejects all established communities – especially nation and state – as spooks, as abstract social bodies and collectivities to whose cause, whether liberal or communist, the egoist is subordinated. The concept of 'society' is the great altar upon which the unique one is routinely sacrificed. In contrast to these spectral forms of community, Stirner introduces his concept of the 'union of egoists' (*Verein von Egoisten*), which is the only form of collective association his philosophy of egoism will countenance (1995: 161). The idea here is of a completely voluntary form of association which the individual egoist joins for his or her own purposes and which poses no binding obligation. Unlike more spectral communities founded upon some imagined essential commonality, which simply absorb the individual into a totality over which they have no power, the 'union of egoists' is consciously willed and determined by singularities who comprise it. Perhaps something like this might be found today in various radical affinity groups, or gatherings such as Occupy, networks such as Anonymous, or even the black bloc – which are not permanent political organizations based on stable identities but, rather, contingent associations of shared intensities. Can we think of the union of egoists as the counterpoint to the Hobbesian body politic? Rather than lonely, fearful individuals compressed claustrophobically into a social body under the alienating gaze of the sovereign, the form of association proposed here is one of shared affects and a joyous intensity, in which singularity is enhanced rather than diminished through its relations with other singularities.

The 'union of egoists', a seemingly paradoxical formulation, should not be taken as a precise model of politics to be followed but, rather, as something revealing the openness, contingency and multiplicity of the political as such. Stirner wants to clear the political field of all fixed and universalizing identities and affirm politics as a site of continual invention and creativity from which multiple forms of subjectivity, action and association can emerge. It suggests a rhizomatic, post-sovereign and post-identity form of political association which defies any logic of representation. The 'union of egoists' is a political figure that allows us to think individual difference and collectivity together, as a kind of multiple body or as multiple singularities.

Stirner's thought provides us with an arsenal of concepts – such as *ownness* and *insurrection* – which are extremely useful to the theorization of radical politics today, and which I shall develop further in following chapters. The emphasis of his thinking is towards the intensification of our autonomy, and his notion of the unique one provides the clearest and most forthright formulation of postanarchist subjectivity.

3

Insurrection

The thematic of ontological anarchy that I have been developing so far demands a reconsideration not only of who we are as subjects, but also of how we engage in political action and, in particular, how we resist the forms of subjectification that have been imposed upon us. If the refusal of fixed and governable identities is central to postanarchism, then political action cannot be conceived in terms of a communication or inclusion of demands within existing representative structures; if 'non-power' is postanarchism's starting point, political action cannot be concerned with the revolutionary seizure of power or the construction of democratic hegemonies. So what form might postanarchist political practice take?

From the riots against police violence in Ferguson, Missouri, to the movements of Occupation around the world, to multiple examples of cyber resistance, radical politics today takes the form of _insurrection_. But what does this mean, exactly? To answer this question, we must consider the difference between insurrection and revolution. Moreover, we must ask ourselves why it

seems so difficult today to think in terms of *revolution* –
if by revolution we understand an event through which
the totality of social and political relations would be
transformed and which, in the Marxist tradition at least,
would be the culmination of the history of human struggle. As I have proposed, we live in the wake of the collapse
of revolutionary grand narratives, in which the idea of a
social totality that can be grasped, overturned and finally
emancipated through revolutionary praxis is no longer
operative. Moreover, the classical revolutionary model
whereby an organized vanguard seizes political control
of the reins of state power, using its coercive apparatuses
to reshape social relations from above, has run aground
on numerous occasions – as indeed the anarchists predicted well over a century ago – and today seems more
and more unlikely. There is no longer a distinct centre
of power, no symbolic Winter Palace to storm. We are
confronted instead with a perplexing field of power relations which take the form of a network rather than a
hierarchy, a field into which we are inserted and with
which we are, in many ways, complicit. This chapter will
therefore be devoted to an exploration of an alternative
insurrectionary understanding of radical politics that I
see as central to postanarchism. My claim will be that
the insurrection is characterized not by a struggle over
power but, rather, by the struggle for autonomous life.

Anarchism and social revolution

It is necessary to retrieve the idea of insurrection –
which is employed increasingly widely today[1] – from

the radical political tradition. Of course, if we under-stand insurrection as a spontaneous uprising against power, then there have been insurrections ever since there were instituted forms of politics. The slave revolts of the ancient world, the peasant uprisings and reli-gious heresies throughout the Middle Ages, and the revolts against autocratic power that characterized the modern period might all be considered insurrec-tions, even if they were brutally suppressed or were co-opted into organized revolutionary movements that founded a new political order. Here it is insufficient, I would argue, to understand insurrection in terms of the distinction – central to modern understandings of sovereignty – between *constitutive* and *constituted* power, or the *pouvoir constituent* and *pouvoir con-stitué* that Abbé Sieyès spoke of in his pamphlet *What is the Third Estate?* (1789). This distinction between the revolutionary source of authority, which lay with the People or Nation, and the constituted political-legal order, which rested on this authority, has been deployed by thinkers on both the radical right, such as Carl Schmitt, and left, such as Antonio Negri. The latter has sought to isolate constituting power (or what he calls *constituent* power) from the political order which it founds, arguing that, as a revolutionary force, it con-tains an insurgent dimension that always exceeds and resists this order, threatening its stability and embody-ing a radically democratic potentiality (see Negri 1999: 10.1) However, as Agamben (1998) has pointed out, constituent revolutionary power, insofar as it always founds a new political and legal order, remains trapped within the paradigm of sovereignty. Instead Agamben proposes something like a *destituent* power, signifying a withdrawal or exodus from the order of sovereignty and law altogether – a form of politics which is not revolutionary but, as I would see it, insurrectionary. I shall say more about this notion of withdrawal later, but we can see how problematic the idea of revolutionary power is: the revolution always aims at the founding of a new political order, a new state, and, as the anarchists argued, it was naïve in the extreme to believe that this would simply 'wither away' of its own accord once the immediate aims of the revolution had been achieved.

Therefore, in contrast to the Marxist 'political revolution' – the strategy of capturing of the state, with all its attendant perils – the anarchists of the nineteenth century proposed the idea of a 'social revolution', which would be aimed at the immediate destruction of state power, a goal which would allow a more genuine transformation of social relations. It is here that Bakunin accused Marx and his followers of merely pursuing a 'politics of a different kind' in wanting to utilize state power to achieve the ends of revolution, whereas the anarchists sought, as he put it, 'the total abolition of politics' (Bakunin 1953: 113–14). The question for Bakunin – and it is still a question for us today, although an increasingly opaque one – is what this 'total abolition of politics' characterized by the destruction of state power would look like. In speaking about preparations for this social revolution, Bakunin calls upon the masses to 'organize their powers apart from and against the state' (ibid.: 377). There is a proposal for the self-organization of the people, not through state representative organizations like political parties, and not even through vanguardist revolutionary parties – both of which remain, in different ways, attached to the apparatus of the state – but through genuinely autonomous, decentralized and participatory mass organizations. This notion of autonomous politics (or *anti-political politics*) 'apart from and against the state' resonates strongly with us today, even more so perhaps than it did in Bakunin's time – we who live during the time of a massive discrediting of representative political institutions, and perhaps of the very notion of state sovereignty itself.

Perhaps, then, the notion of insurrection as an autonomous form of political mobilization and practice which sets itself apart from the state – which does not seek state power for itself but actually embodies its dissolution – was already implicit in the anarchist idea of social revolution. Yet, to the extent that there is a difference between these two concepts, it lies not in the question of the instrumentalization of state power (both concepts reject this) but rather in the imagining of the social field. As I showed in a previous chapter, the anarchists of the nineteenth century saw social relations as embodying an underlying rationality and morality – conveyed for instance in Kropotkin's notion of mutual aid, which he saw as an innate natural instinct. This meant that the revolution against the state – the social revolution – could be seen in terms of society, as a body, throwing off this oppressive and artificial encumbrance, whereupon free, voluntary forms of community, which were always immanent, would come to the fore and spontaneously replace state institutions. This also allowed the revolution to be seen as a coming event which would transform society once and for all, opening the way to a vastly superior and more cooperative form of social organization. As I have suggested, however, we can no longer rely on the idea of a coherent, rational social body as a foundation for politics – the social field is much too differentiated and complex; nor can we imagine a revolutionary event that will solve all the problems of power. As the insurrectionary anarchist Alfredo Bonanno suggests, it is no longer possible, in the conditions of late modern post-industrial societies, to have these sureties. Here he proposes a form of politics which is different, on the one hand, from riots, which are disorganized, violent and fragmented, and, on the other, from the old model of revolution. The insurrection relies on informal groups of anarchists, organized on the basis of affinity, who intervene in specific situations without these actions being overdetermined by the idea of the immanent revolution – in other words, without the expectation that such actions will lead to the social revolution: 'Informal organisation, therefore, that establishes a simple discourse presented without grand objectives, and without claiming, as many do, that every intervention must lead to social revolution, otherwise what sort of anarchists would we be?' (Bonanno 1988: 28). Understanding anarchist political practices in this way frees them from a certain revolutionary dogmatism, allowing them to intervene in situations which are necessarily contingent and opaque. Although Bonanno would no doubt abhor the term, this insurrectionary attitude that he describes points to a distinction that could be made between an anarchist and *postanarchist* conception of political action.

Insurrection

The insurrection of the self

In the previous chapter, I developed, mostly through Stirner's philosophy of egoism, the idea of singularity as a way of understanding autonomous forms of subjectivation that are emerging today. I suggested that singularities are not identities, and they resist the very representational logic of liberalism and identity politics; indeed, they imply an insurrection against fixed identities. In order to understand this revolt of singularities, we can turn once again to Stirner and to his particular notion of insurrection or *Empörung* (Uprising), which he distinguishes carefully from revolution:

> Revolution and insurrection must not be looked upon as synonymous. The former consists in an overturning of conditions, of the established condition or *status*, the state or society, and is accordingly a *political* or *social* act; the latter has indeed for its unavoidable consequence a transformation of circumstances, yet does not start from it but from men's discontent with themselves, is not an armed rising but a rising of individuals, a getting up without regard to the *arrangements* that spring from it. The Revolution aimed at new arrangements; insurrection leads us no longer to *let* ourselves be arranged, but to arrange ourselves, and sets no glittering hopes on 'institutions'. It is not a fight against the established, since, if it prospers, the established collapses of itself; it is only a working forth of me out of the established. (1995: 279–80; emphasis in original)

The revolution works to transform external social and political conditions and institutions – in this sense, there is little difference between the Marxist

53

'political' revolution and anarchist 'social' revolution. The insurrection, by contrast, is aimed at one's own self-transformation (it starts 'from men's discontent with themselves'); it involves placing oneself *above* external conditions and constraints, whereupon these constraints simply disintegrate. It starts from the affirmation of the self, and the political consequences flow from this. As we can see, the insurrection, unlike the revolution, is radically anti-institutional – not necessarily in the sense of seeking to get rid of all institutions, as this would lead simply to different kinds of institutions, but rather in the sense of asserting our power over institutions and, indeed, our autonomy from them. The insurrection is an affirmation of the autonomy and singularity of the individual – of his or her own power over himself. It suggests a micro-political transformation of the self in its relation to power, such that we are able to extricate ourselves from systems of power and our dependency on them, even our desire for them (it is a 'working forth of me out of the established'; ibid.: 280).

We can see, then, that this notion of insurrection is radically different from most understandings of radical political action. It eschews the idea of an overarching project of emancipation or social transformation; freedom is not the end goal of the insurrection but, rather, its starting point. In other words, the insurrection starts not with the desire to change external conditions which might be said to oppress the individual but, rather, with the affirmation of the self over these conditions, as if to say: *power exists but it is not my concern; I refuse to let it constrain me or have any effect on me; I refuse power's power over me.* While some might claim that this is a naïve idealism that leads to political quietism – indeed, this was precisely the thrust of Marx and Engels's crude attack on Stirner in *The German Ideology* – I would argue that the consequences of this position are profoundly radical. We must consider the extent to which power is sustained by our interactions with it – even at times by our hostility towards it; and if we manage to distance and disentangle ourselves from power, and from the identities and subjectivities which power imposes upon us, then power becomes an empty husk, a dry and cracked shell which crumbles into itself. So, rather than a revolutionary project which sets itself the goal of liberating people from power – and which risks merely imposing upon them another kind of power in its place – the insurrection allows people to constitute their own freedom or, as Stirner puts it, their 'ownness', by first reclaiming their own self – that is to say, reclaiming their autonomy. We might say, then, that the insurrection is the political articulation of ontological anarchy: a form of praxis which is not overdetermined by a project or *telos*, but which simply assumes and puts into practice the freedom that we already have.

What Stirner's notion of insurrection alerts us to is the extent to which we are complicit – through our self-abdication – with the systems of power that we see as dominating. Perhaps we need to understand power not as a substance or a thing, but as a relationship which we forge and renew everyday through our actions and our relations with others. As the anarchist Gustav Landauer (2010) put it, 'The state is a social relationship; a certain way of people relating to one another. It can be destroyed by creating new social relationships;

i.e., by people relating to one another differently.' Again, the emphasis here is not so much on the revolutionary seizure or destruction of the external system of power as on a micro-political transformation of the self and its relation to others and the creation of alternative and more autonomous relations – the result of which is the disintegration of state power. We can perhaps speak of an *internalized* insurrection, an insurrection that goes to the roots of our subjectivity, even our psyche, before it is turned outwards. Perhaps we might see insurrections as a form of radical psychotherapy[2] in which, through a reflection on our dependencies on power, our desires to dominate and be dominated – which are after all two sides of the same coin – and our pathological relations with others, we are brought to a state of self-affirmation where we realize that power's hold over us is basically an illusion. I will return to this point in a later chapter.

It should be clear by now that the insurrection is not the organization of a counter-power or counter-hegemony, to speak in Gramscian terms. It is not the consolidation of the forces of civil society into a coherent political bloc which seeks to take over state power. Counter-power always becomes simply another form of power. Rather, the insurrection signifies a withdrawal from the game of power and counter-power altogether – indeed, an *indifference* to power. Its focus is on the transformation of the self and its immediate relation to others, and on the development of autonomous ways of living which seek to avoid the trap that power has laid for us. The insurrection is the relational space of freedom that is opened up when we reclaim and affirm ourselves, outside of any institutionalized form or any predetermined *telos*.

The new Cynics

The insurrection is a withdrawal not only from the political field – that is to say, the formal field of political institutions and systems of power – but also from the economic field. It signifies a refusal of the life of debt, consumption and financial control that has turned the existence of many around the world into one of misery, precariousness and servitude. This economic and political system is now being confronted with the naked life that it has produced. One of the striking and powerful aspects of the Occupy movement was the unexpected appearance of people in public places – masses of people symbolizing, in their sheer physical presence, their nakedness, vulnerability and precarity. In setting up encampments, and living and sleeping in public squares, people showed their defiance of or, rather, indifference to power and their willingness to use official public spaces precisely in the way that they are not supposed to be used – as *public* spaces.

Yet, I would argue that this reclamation of public space and public life – the right of ordinary people to practise politics – is quite different from the Arendtian notion of politics as appearance in the public domain, which relies so fundamentally on the division, central to the ancient Greek polis, between the public and private realms.[3] As we know, for Arendt, the life proper to politics – the *vita activa* – must be carefully distinguished from the life of labour, economic necessity and the private sphere of the *oikos* (see Arendt 1999).[4] There is with Arendt, as well as in a different sense with Schmitt, an affirmation of the imaginary dimension of 'the political' as a sovereign and sacred space of collective human activity autonomous from the market. This separation of the sovereign space of politics from the domain of the market, of the public from the private sphere, no longer seems possible, if indeed it ever was. Moreover, it presupposes an exclusion of subjects and ways of life deemed not worthy of the polis.[5] By contrast, the insurrections that we see today stage the intrusion of naked life – the life of necessity and survival – into the political realm, the realm of collective action and decision-making, thus collapsing the public/private division.

Here we are reminded of a very different conception of a political life symbolized by the curious figure of Diogenes the Cynic, who lived his life openly and publicly in the agora, sleeping naked in streets and marketplaces of ancient Athens. The scandal of his existence was to dissolve the distinction between life and politics, between the private hearth and the public square. Michel Foucault, in his final lectures at the Collège de France in 1984, reflected on Diogenes as an example of the genuine philosophical life, in which the courage of truth and the ethics of existence were embodied in every gesture and act, in one's daily life and activities. The ethical life was necessarily a scandalous life and an ascetic life, a life lived in public in the full scorn of society – the life of a dog who sleeps in the streets. The ethical life was also a militant life in the sense that it pitted itself against the norms, mores and institutions of existing society and sought to break radically with them. The highly individualistic figure of the Cynic philosopher, in his radical otherness, disrupts the boundaries of the polis and affirms his own sovereign existence in an agonistic contestation of its collective mores. The Cynic seeks, and indeed embodies in his own violently ascetic and militant style of living, an *other life* and an *other world* within the existing world (see Foucault 2011: 287).[6] The lesson of Diogenes, then, may be that, to do politics differently, we must learn to live differently and embody politics in life and life in politics. This is what Foucault was perhaps getting at with the notion of *bios philosophikos*: 'The *bios philosophikos* as straight life is the human being's animality taken up as a challenge, practiced as an exercise, and thrown in the face of others as a scandal' (ibid.: 265; emphasis in original). Perhaps we could see in the movements of Occupation, in the encampments that quietly and joyfully laid siege to power, a glimpse of a new kind of political and philosophical life. The beautiful, simple gesture of sleeping and living on the streets, without shame or fear, signifies, like the setting up of revolutionary barricades in the nineteenth century, a real moment of rupture in our world.

What we can also take from this is the potential power that lies in a certain ascetic attitude to one's life. While this might be an attitude that has been forced upon many of us by economic necessity, it can nevertheless form the basis of a new sensibility and ethos, and a new mode of subjectivity, central to which is the refusal of unnecessary consumption and the desire for a simpler way of living. The only way that we can free ourselves ultimately from the economic system that enslaves us – through debt and endless, meaningless work – is if we come to no longer desire it, if we refuse the fetishism of commodities and disinvest our desires from the capitalist way of life and from the psychic economy of guilt that arises with constant indebtedness. Part of this would be a rethinking of the whole ideology of economic growth and asserting the priorities of human and ecological sustainability, even embracing the idea of de-growth (décroissance).[7] Franco Berardi talks about the importance of 'slowness' as a response to the constant capitalist imperative of growth and acceleration, particularly in the European context: 'The coming European insurrection will not be an insurrection of energy, but an insurrection of slowness, withdrawal, and exhaustion. It will be the autonomization of the collective body and soul from the exploitation of speed and competition' (2012: 68).

Yet, while this attitude might be born of exhaustion, more significantly, it points to the exhaustion of a certain way of life and therefore the possibility of alternative ways of living – a realization that provokes a new energy of invention and innovation. The affirmation of the 'poor life' at the same time involves an active experimentation in alternative non-capitalistic forms of economic exchange, based on an ethos and practices of generosity, conviviality and the sharing of common resources. Glimpses of these practices were apparent in the various forms of voluntary cooperation and self-management that we find so frequently today – in alternative economies, forms of exchange and practices of 'commoning' which are visible all around us if we choose to look, and which are emerging in the shadow of the neoliberal economic crisis – from barter economies, food cooperatives and community banking to organic farming and factory reoccupations. These experiments, while born of necessity, at the same time are an expression of a desire for an autonomous life and non-commodified life – a life reclaimed from the control of dominant political and financial systems.

Ownness

What is an autonomous life? Autonomy is usually associated with notions of self-government and self-determination. Of course, there are many understandings of autonomy in political theory: the idea is commonly associated with liberal conceptions of individual freedom realizable within a certain type of regime based on rights and the rule of law or with the Kantian notion of moral autonomy, which refers to the rational capacity to give to oneself the universal moral law rather than being influenced by the wills of others. My own conception of autonomy, which I will outline in greater detail in a later chapter, is rather different from this and is heavily influenced by Stirner's conception of ownness. To understand ownness we must distinguish it from freedom, which appears to us today an increasingly elusive and ambiguous concept. For Stirner, freedom is another one of those universal ideals, or 'spooks', an empty abstraction to which we are sacrificed, which alienates and disempowers us. The problem with freedom is that its proclaimed universality disguises a particular position of power – it is always someone's idea of freedom that is imposed coercively upon others: 'The craving for a *particular* freedom always includes the purpose of a new *domination*' (Stirner 1995: 145). So, to pose the question of freedom as a universal aspiration is always to pose the question of which particular order of power imposes this freedom, thereby inevitably limiting and constraining its radical possibilities. Therefore, freedom must be left to the 'unique one' to determine for him- or herself. It should be seen as ongoing elaboration of individual autonomy rather than a general political and social goal – freedom as a singular practice, unique to the individual, rather than a universally proclaimed ideal and aspiration. Freedom, in other words, must be divested of its abstractions and brought down to the level of the unique one.

This is why Stirner prefers the term 'ownness' to 'freedom', ownness implying self-ownership or self-mastery – in other words, a kind of autonomy, which means *more* than freedom because it gives one the *freedom to be free*, the freedom to define one's own singular path of freedom: 'Ownness *created* a new *freedom*' (1995: 147). Rather than conforming to a universal ideal, something which is so often accompanied with the most terrible forms of coercion, ownness is a project of open-ended creation and invention, in which new forms of freedom can be discovered. As Stirner says: 'My *own* I am at all times and under all circumstances, if I know how to have myself and do not throw myself away on others. To be free is something that I cannot truly *will*, because I cannot make it, cannot create it' (ibid.: 143). Ownness is a way of restoring to the individual his or her capacity for freedom, of reminding the individual that he is already free in an ontological sense, rather than seeing freedom as a universal goal to be attained for humanity. If freedom is disempowering and illusory, ownness, in Stirner's view, is a way of making freedom concrete and real and, moreover, of revealing to the unique one what he had long forgotten – his own power: 'I am free from what I am rid of, owner of what I have in my *power* or what I *control*' (ibid.).

At the same time, we could say that ownness, or autonomy, is not confined to a strictly individualistic endeavour and is something that can be practised associatively, in collaboration with others. I have already spoken of Stirner's union of egoists as one possible way of thinking about autonomous collective action. However, the forms of solidarity that emerge as part of the insurrection are still grounded in the 'egoistic' desires of the singularities who participate in it. In other words, cooperation and what Kropotkin would call 'mutual aid' are engaged in not out of some sense of self-sacrifice and obligation but, on the contrary, out of one's own 'selfish' sense of joy and pleasure, which is intensified through one's relations with others. As Berardi puts it, 'solidarity is not about you, it's about me' (2012: 54). So, the postanarchist insurrection is not a Cause for which one sacrifices oneself – the last thing radical politics needs today are any more sad, pious militants, whose apparent selflessness often masks the most vicious sensibilities. Rather, as a politics of ownness, the insurrection is a movement of joy, conviviality and the happiness experienced in being together with others.

Insurrection

Prefiguration

The importance that I have placed here on emotional affect touches on one of the central features of insurrectionary politics today – that of prefiguration, which refers to the idea that political action should already embody the ethical form and principles of the type of society one hopes to build. Prefiguration, therefore, signals a refusal of strategic politics in which means are sacrificed to revolutionary ends. This approach to politics was evident in recent insurrections such as Occupy, which deliberately sought to ward off Power by establishing horizontal and participatory structures and decision-making practices. Indeed, prefigurative politics has for some time been a defining feature of global anti-capitalism (see Graeber 2004). Of course, prefiguration has always been closely associated with anarchism, whose critique of Marxism and Marxist-Leninism was made precisely on the grounds that their exponents were prepared to use authoritarian and militaristic means to achieve the revolution, means which would condemn post-revolutionary society to a replication of the authoritarian and hierarchical institutions they sought to liberate us from. For the anarchists, by contrast, the revolution would be libertarian in form as well as aim, and principles of freedom, equality and self-organization must not be sacrificed to strategic calculations and political ends – for this would be the very betrayal of the ideals of the revolution. This emphasis on prefiguration has made anarchism perhaps the most ethical of all the radical political traditions.

However, we need to consider what prefiguration can mean today. I would suggest that prefiguration has two main implications in the context of contemporary insurrections. Firstly, there is the idea – which I regard as central to ontological anarchism – that the insurrection takes place in the immediacy of the present, in the here and now, without being determined by a particular future end or *telos*.[8] Any future arrangements which might emerge from the insurrection are always contingent; the emphasis is, rather, on the present form taken by the insurrection and on seeing the insurrection as an expression of ownness, the reclamation of the self. Secondly, prefigurative practices should be regarded as what Foucault would call 'practices of freedom' – in other words, elaborations of ethical practices and a constant work on oneself in order to invent subjectivities and relationships which are self-governing and no longer enthralled to power. Such practices are contingent, may take different forms in different contexts, and are without guarantees. They have to be experimented with and constantly reinvented.

We can no longer sustain the idea, present in classical anarchism, of the uprising of an already constituted rational and ethical social body against the external encumbrance of power. As I have suggested, this social totality no longer exists, which is why contemporary insurrections need to invent new forms of solidarity and being-in-common. The commonly invoked idea of a movement of 'global civil society' is therefore somewhat misguided. Rather, insurrections embody a certain rupturing of 'civil society'. This does not mean, of course, that existing traditions, relations and practices are automatically and violently discarded; I am by no means invoking a Jacobin logic which insists that the past must be erased and the slate wiped clean. This is precisely the revolutionary mind-set – which asserts the sovereignty of political will over the complexity of social relations – I want to get away from. Indeed, many traditions and practices, particularly those aimed at conserving the natural environment, are worth preserving and fighting for. My point, rather, is that insurrections can no longer be ontologically grounded in pre-existing social relations. Indeed, we could say that they place themselves in a certain situation of war with 'society' and aim at the dissolution of existing social bonds and ties. There is not too little society – as communitarians of all stripes like to claim – but rather too much. We are hemmed in from all sides by this 'spook', to use Stirner's term. The insurrection, as a figure for contemporary radical forms of politics, therefore involves the creation of alternative forms of non-essential existence, based not on some pre-ordained ideal or image of society but on the desires of the singularities who comprise it.

But let us not, at the same time, be too sanguine here. Insurrections carry enormous risks – of violent repression, of the dissipation of their energies, or of becoming themselves violent and authoritarian. I will discuss the question of violence in greater depth in chapter 4. At the present time, it seems there is a very real opacity and ambiguity surrounding the insurrection and its future. Indeed, if we look around us today we are perhaps more likely to see 'insurrections' that take a completely perverted form – seeking to violently recompose the social body and alive with populist, racist and fundamentalist energies. Fascism remains their eternal temptation. Autonomous insurrection can mean many things today – and no doubt we need to be clearer about the micro-political and ethical dimension of autonomy, beyond the simple idea of the rejection of state institutions. Yet, my contention is that such ambiguities cannot be resolved either by returning to the old idea of Revolution or by embracing the institutions of parliamentary democracy. Rather, the postanarchist insurrection must stake out its ground, ethically and politically, on an uncertain and shifting terrain.

4

Violence against Violence

To speak of insurrection, as I did in the previous chapter, inevitably brings to light the question of violence and its ambiguous relationship to radical politics. As I suggested, insurrection is a kind of social war or, rather, a war against the imagined totality and unity of society, even if – and this is the hope – it is essentially non-violent. Indeed, radical politics in general always implies a certain violence in rupturing existing social and political conditions. However, the question of violence presents a unique ethical problem for anarchism and, indeed, postanarchism, especially with regard to their emphasis on prefigurative politics. While anarchism in the past has been no stranger to violence – from the violent 'propaganda of the deed' during the nineteenth century to full-scale military campaigns during the Russian and Spanish civil wars in the twentieth century – there is at the same time the ethical problematization of violence as a coercive and authoritarian relationship which centrally contradicts anarchist principles. Anarchism has been characterized by both violent and non-violent

68

resistance to power, and it is known as much for its pacifist traditions – Thoreau and Tolstoy – as for political assassinations.

Postanarchism today must therefore wrestle with a very real tension: on the one hand, there is the recognition that violence is ethically as well as politically untenable. Not only does violence coerce and dominate others, violating their autonomy in the worst possible way, but violent resistance against power risks an even greater and more devastating counter-violence; violence against the state always plays to the state's advantage, and any kind of armed uprising will be easily crushed. At the same time, as an agonistic and insurrectionary form of politics, postanarchism confronts practices of domination and state violence and therefore engages in what might be seen as *violence against violence.* Moreover, the use of violence in self-defence would be entirely justifiable from a postanarchist position; and, as anyone knows who has ever been to a demonstration that has 'turned ugly', as the media likes to say, much of the violence of the crowd is a defensive reaction – one could say a counter-violence – to the violent provocations of the police, who often deliberately inflame the situation. In grappling with this ethical dilemma over the use of force, activists have developed very innovative and effective techniques of civil disobedience or what could be called 'non-violent warfare' (see Graeber 2002). Moreover, while the insurrection, at least in my understanding, declares war on political institutions by placing itself above them – after all, what could be a more violent gesture in the eyes of the state than people affirming their indifference to it? – it is at the same time distinct from a revolution in the sense that it is not an uprising that aims to seize power through force of arms: in other words, the insurrection is 'non-violent' precisely in the sense that it does not turn violence into an instrument for the conquest of power. Insofar as it is indifferent to power, it has no need for guns and explosives.

Nevertheless, as the world around us seems to be exploding into violence at the moment – something which I have no wish to add to – I believe it is important to be clearer about how radical politics understands violence and its relationship to it. In this chapter, I aim to develop a postanarchist approach to the question of violence by drawing on the thought of Georges Sorel and Walter Benjamin, both of whom I read in a distinctly anarchistic way. In both thinkers we find an understanding of violence as an ontologically anarchic form of action – as pure means without a specific end or *telos*. The challenge here is to develop a conception of *counter-violence* which allows us to reflect more carefully on the political and ethical contours of radical political action today.

Anarchism and social warfare

We need first to examine anarchism's rather paradoxical relationship to violence. While there is, as I said, an ethical reservation about the use of violence against persons, anarchism nevertheless maintains a close proximity to the notion of war. This might be understood in two senses. Firstly, there is the claim that centralized political power, no matter how it is dressed up, whether it is democratic or autocratic, stands in a relationship of war with society: state power, it is argued, is not based on consent but is a violently imposed form of domination which intervenes in social relations in irrational and destructive ways. So, behind the various illusions and justificatory ideologies of democratic consent and the social contract, there is only conquest and violent domination. As Kropotkin's counter-history reveals, the state is a system of power and accumulation that has been imposed through warfare rather than emerging through rational agreement (see Kropotkin 1987: 37). The state is a form of organized violence, whose domination is established through the conquest of territory and the destruction of pre-existing social relationships. Secondly, if the state is a war machine, it can only be confronted with another war machine, that of the social revolution. Here, the revolution against the state is conceived in terms of war: 'Revolution means war, and that implies the destruction of men and things', thundered Bakunin (1953: 372). However, while this might seem like an endorsement or acceptance of wholesale violence, the anarchist social revolution would liberate people from politically instituted forms of violence:

The Social Revolution must put an end to the old system of organization based upon violence, giving full liberty to the masses, groups, communes, and associations, and likewise to individuals themselves, and destroying once and for all the historic cause of all violences . . . (Ibid.: 372)

So, in this sense, the anarchist social revolution might be understood as a form of counter-violence, a *violence against violence*. The violence of the state – a violence that is much more excessive in any case than any form of violence opposed to it – can only be met with a counter-violence; but here violence is transformed into a kind of radical non-violence. This is not to confuse it with peace, because, as the anarchist analysis shows, the peaceful coexistence achieved by the state is only a crystallization of violence and conquest. Rather, in order to unmask the violence upon which it rests, the state can only be confronted with another kind of violence. So, it is not a question of whether or not a revolution against state power will be violent – against such overwhelming violence and power, it cannot be anything other than violent. Rather it is a question of whether it is possible to have a form of violence that, in seeking the abolition of power, at the same time seeks the abolition of violence itself. It is not clear, then, how exactly the violence of the social revolution should be understood: while it may indeed involve real instances of violence, it is at the same time a mass action aimed against violence. The essential point here is that the transcendence of violence is only possible, at the same time, through invoking and drawing upon the language and the symbolism of war. Indeed, the idea of war is something that, at some level, animates all forms of radical politics. Perhaps we can say that a radical critique of existing social and political structures presupposes the possibility of war, in the same way that Carl Schmitt (1996) believed that the political opposition between friend and enemy depended on the possibility of violence.

Violence against Violence

Sorel's proletarian general strike: mythic war

Yet, if violence against violence is a central theme in anarchism, and indeed in postanarchism, then surely it is insufficient merely to accept the instrumental use of violence in the pursuit of ends of revolution. Violence against violence must mean something more than this – perhaps, as I suggested, the sublimation of violence into different forms of struggle that retain the language and symbolism of war yet refuse, or wherever possible avoid, real violence against persons.[1] Someone who can help us think about this is Georges Sorel, who, in his Syndicalist phase at least, developed a radical understanding of insurrectionary violence which, I would argue, has important parallels with and implications for postanarchism.

In *Reflections on Violence* (1961) (*Réflexions sur la violence*, 1908), Sorel considers the prospects for class struggle and workers' revolution at the turn of the twentieth century. The chief obstacle to the revolution, he argues, is the moral degeneration of the proletariat, its loss of class identity and its subsumption within the bourgeois moral universe. Proletarian moral and political energy has been dissipated through the internalization of bourgeois values, as well as through the obfuscating role of socialist politicians, whose function was to incorporate the working class into representative structures of the capitalist state and the 'social peace' – a kind of corporatist consensus between labour and capital which merely shrouded capitalism in humanitarian and social democratic illusions. It is as if Sorel predicted here the sad fate of social democracy and the

73

ignominious politics of the Third Way nearly a century before its time.

Violence, Sorel argues, has an important role to play in restoring the political and moral vitality of the working class by sharpening class distinctions which had hitherto been blurred. Violence is what allows the proletariat to overcome its position of 'decadence', to spurn the hypocritical humanitarian overtures of the capitalists and socialist politicians, and to rediscover its 'egoism' (Sorel 1961: 90–1).[2] In other words, violence allows the proletariat to affirm its autonomous class identity and values in opposition to that great agent of 'decadence' and 'incapacity', the modern state.

But what kind of violence is Sorel talking about here? We must pay close attention to his idea of the proletarian general strike and his understanding of the function of myth. The proletarian general strike is a form of revolutionary direct action engaged in by workers themselves, without the mediation of the state and political parties. It is at the same time a kind of myth, a myth of war – specifically class war, whose centrality to Marxist theory Sorel wanted to restore. The general strike embodies the symbolism of a battlefield – it enacts the drama of a decisive battle between the proletariat and the bourgeoisie. The drama of war has the effect of galvanizing the energy and passions of the working class. Sorel described the myth as 'a body of images capable of evoking instinctively all the sentiments which correspond to the different manifestations of the war undertaken by Socialism against modern society' (1961: 127). The myth of the general strike might therefore be understood as a sort of *mise en scène*, in which all the emotional and political energy of previous strikes and workers' actions are concentrated to a point of maximum intensity, something that produces militant and heroic affects in workers, imbuing them with warrior-like virtues of courage and self-discipline, as well as a new-found vitality: 'appealing to their painful memories of particular conflicts, it colours with an intense life all the details of the composition presented to consciousness' (ibid.).

Does this curious idea of the general strike as a mythic war have any currency today in our post-revolutionary era, in which working-class identity and class consciousness are much more opaque than in Sorel's time, and in which a millenarian confrontation between two social forces seems difficult to imagine? There are, nevertheless, some important lessons here. I have discussed the emotional intensity – the affective state of joy and conviviality – that animates the insurrection. It seems to me that what radical politics lacks today is an energy and vitality – something that this sort of direct action might inspire. Sorel's vitalist thought, influenced by Henri Bergson, can help us to think about a notion of political intensity that is distinct from the Schmittian matrix of enmity which seeks only to energize the sovereign. As we shall see, this Sorelian notion of political intensity generated through the violence of the general strike embodies the radical dissolution of the state. Furthermore, the general strike conveys the idea of direct action in the immediacy of the present, in the here and now – action is understood here not as a means to an end but as an end in itself. For Sorel, the violence of the general strike is the violence of *pure means*. This is similar to the notion of ontological anarchy, in which action is determined not by a particular programme or *telos* – some utopian future, an idea Sorel also rejected – but by the immediacy and contingency of the present situation.

This notion of pure means or means without end is also reflected in Sorel's understanding of political subjectivation. Even though he is working within the Marxist class framework, the proletarian subject, paradoxically, does not precede the general strike but is actually constituted by it; the working class discovers who it is through revolutionary action itself. There is a non-essentialist – one could say post-identity – understanding of political subjectivity operating here which is quite close to postanarchist theory, even though postanarchism no longer retains the Marxian class categories. Sorel's notion of political subjectivation also points to the importance of virtue – a warrior-like courage, nobility and self-discipline. Just as the Christian martyrs distinguished themselves through their fortitude, self-discipline and commitment to moral struggle, so the proletariat must learn to discipline itself and acquire its own morality and nobility; it must develop, as Sorel puts it, '*habits of liberty* with which the bourgeoisie are no longer acquainted' (1961: 88; emphasis in original). While Sorel's moralism might seem a strange fit with anarchist politics, it nevertheless points to the need to cultivate certain ethics and virtues for political struggle and autonomous existence. Especially important here is the notion of discipline, which is not imposed by some external agent – such as a revolutionary vanguard or supreme Legislator that guides and shapes the will of the masses – but is the discipline one cultivates and imposes freely upon oneself. I will pursue this idea in a later chapter. But it seems to me that freedom or ownness, as I have chosen to call it (following Stirner), is something that does not necessarily arise spontaneously but comes about only through practices of self-disciplining such that one's dependencies on power and familiar patterns and habits of obedience and consumption are broken: perhaps we could call this a *discipline of indiscipline*. Indeed, Sorel's insistence on morality and even a certain kind of purity was in order to wean the proletariat off its dependence, not only on the state and its agents of representation, but particularly on the moral culture of the bourgeoisie and the capitalist system. Perhaps, in this sense, a certain kind of 'puritanism' – I have spoken of ascetic values in the previous chapter – would be necessary to enable us to detach ourselves from the culture of consumerism and the capitalist circuits of desire in which we are so thoroughly immersed. We have to remember that capitalism, and neoliberal capitalism in particular, governs us through our 'freedom' – our *freedom* to consume, to work and to obey – and we can break with this system and develop alternative and more genuine practices of freedom only through a certain kind of self-discipline. As Sorel suggests, liberty is a new *habit* that we are yet to learn.

Autonomy and violence

The proletarian general strike is the event that endows the proletariat with the capacity for freedom or, as I would put it, 'ownness'. This is largely because it is a form of autonomous direct action without any agent of mediation or direction: the workers in this scenario emancipate themselves from capitalism and the state by directly seizing control of – we could say occupying – the means of production, without working through the state and without coming under the political direction of a vanguard party. In this sense, the kind of revolutionary action Sorel has in mind is much closer to anarchism than Socialism or Marxist-Leninism: 'It is impossible that there should be the slightest misunderstanding between the Syndicalists and official Socialists on this question: the latter, of course, speak of breaking up everything, but they attack men in power rather than power itself' (1961: 117). In other words, whereas the Syndicalists destroy power, the Socialists seek to possess and command it – and this simply reproduces state power. In this sense, we could say that the reformist and revolutionary wings of the Socialist tradition work within the same statist paradigm, the difference being simply the means used to achieve control of the state. While Sorel admired both Bernstein and Lenin, they would be, in his analysis, on the same side.

Sorel therefore proposes an important distinction between the *proletarian general strike*, which embodies the radical dissolution of state power through the affirmation of workers' autonomy and direct action – and which in this sense is anti-political – and the *political general strike*, which is orchestrated by Socialist politicians and trade unions, and which is intended not to destroy state power but to exercise a greater political control over it and to wring concessions from the capitalist class – something which, in Sorel's eyes, only increases the proletariat's impotence and dependency. The two forms of action are completely different, not simply in their aims but also in the sense that the political general strike is a form of strategic action which instrumentalizes the threat of proletarian violence in order to gain concessions and political advantage, while the proletarian general strike can be considered as *pure means* without specific ends. The dissolution of the state is not the strategic aim as such but is, rather, embodied and symbolized in the very action itself. Once again, there is a clear parallel here with a postanarchist conception of politics. As we can see, the idea of autonomy is central to the proletarian general strike: it has nothing to do with bargaining with the system for better conditions but is, rather, the complete disengagement of workers from the state and capitalism through the cultivation of alternative social practices, subjectivities and ethical relations. It seems to me that, today, there is a need to think again in terms of a general strike, which would imply a withdrawal or exodus from our normal patterns of work, consumption and obedience.

Importantly, these two forms of action that Sorel outlines correspond to two different understandings of violence. For Sorel, precisely because the proletarian general strike avoids the temptations of power – because it seeks autonomy from the state rather than wanting to control it – the violence it invokes translates, paradoxically, into radical non-violence. The battlefield on which proletarian violence is enacted is a symbolic one, and militaristic action is to be understood metaphorically. The violence here is symbolic and ethical, a kind of stylized, gestural confrontation with the enemy which imbues the worker with a warrior-like nobility and virtue, yet which does not involve real physical violence:

> they are purely and simply acts of war; they have the value of military demonstrations, and serve to mark the separation of classes. Everything in war is carried on without hatred and without the spirit of revenge; in war the vanquished are not killed; non-combatants are not made to bear the consequences of the disappointments which the armies may have experienced on the fields of battle; force is then displayed according to its own nature, without ever professing to borrow anything from the judicial proceedings which society sets up against criminals. (Sorel 1961: 115)

This last point is a reference to the political and legal violence of the state, a form of violence which is infinitely bloodier than proletarian violence. Here Sorel has in mind the Jacobin Terror in France in the early 1790s – the violent proscriptions and persecutions of the enemies of the revolution at the hands of the new revolutionary leadership. His point, therefore, is that forms of revolutionary action which aim to seize control of state power are much more likely to result in real violence, whereas it is precisely because proletarian autonomy wants no truck with the state at all that it manages to avoid bloodshed and sublimate its violence into a symbolic war. Indeed, Sorel refers to state-legal violence as bourgeois *force* and reserves the term *violence* for the chivalrous and heroic form of proletarian warfare described above. He says:

> the term *violence* should be employed only for acts of revolt; we should say, therefore, that the object of force

is to impose a certain social order in which the minority governs, while violence tends to the destruction of that order. The middle class have used force since the beginning of modern times, while the proletariat now reacts against the middle classes and against the State by violence. (Ibid.: 172; emphasis in original)

We can conclude from this that what makes violence *violent* in the real sense – what turns violence into *force*, as Sorel puts it – is its *state-ification*; in other words, force entails real bloodshed because it uses the mechanisms of state power to impose a certain social order. It is not merely to say that the state is an instrument of violence – and will always be the most violent of instruments due to its capacity to be so – but more that the logic of statism, the logic by which a certain order is imposed coercively upon the world, is what produces untold violence. Therein lies the danger for all revolutionary projects, bourgeois or socialist, which seek to control the reins of the state; the history of this kind of revolutionary path is soaked in blood. By contrast, the violence of autonomous revolution – or, as I would call it, insurrection – because it distances itself from the state and seeks to dissolve its power, transforms itself into a kind a symbolic and ethical violence of rupture. The insurrection might be said to be a violence against an existing set of social relations rather than violence against persons.

Benjamin and the 'Critique of Violence'

In further developing this notion of non-violent violence, we can turn to Walter Benjamin's famous and enigmatic essay 'Critique of Violence' ('Zur Kritik der Gewalt', 1921), a text which is impossible to understand other than in the context of Sorel's thought.[3] I would also suggest that Benjamin's thinking and his critique of legal violence and state sovereignty has clear relevance to postanarchism. The problem Benjamin addresses here is how to develop an ethical critique of violence which does not simply reproduce it. His point is that law cannot serve as an effective basis for this critique, because law itself is inextricably bound to violence. Nor can we make any coherent distinction between legal and illegal, legitimate and illegitimate violence. The law always articulates itself through a violence which both preserves its boundaries and exceeds them; and violence always establishes a new law. Violence is present in the very founding of a new legal system, and this violence haunts its foundations and structures. Benjamin's analysis of legal authority is very similar to that of anarchism, which unmasks the violent foundations of law and sovereignty. He gives the example of military violence, which establishes a new legal system in the place of the old through the signing of a peace treaty following a conquest, as well as that of the death penalty, which signifies law's ultimate sovereignty over life, and whose purpose is not so much the punishment of those who transgress the law as the affirmation of law as life's inescapable fate. Benjamin's point here is that law always instantiates itself – founding and reaffirming itself – through violence. Violence brings law into being, breathes life into it, gives it vitality: 'violence, violence crowned by fate, is the origin of the law' (Benjamin 1996: 242).

Violence against Violence

Benjamin introduces a conceptual distinction between 'lawmaking' (*rechtsetzend*) violence and 'law-preserving' (*rechtserhaltend*) violence: the violence that establishes a new law and the violence that enforces existing laws. Benjamin's point is to show how these two forms of violence ultimately collapse into each other, so that there is a continual oscillation between the two. The key example he gives here is that of the police, in which is combined, 'in a kind of spectral mixture', these two forms of violence (Benjamin 1996: 242). The use of police violence for the purpose of law enforcement is obviously law-preserving. Yet it is also lawmaking, because the police act at the very limits of the law and have the authority to determine how the law is applied in certain situations. The police often act outside the law, or at its margins, in order to enforce it. The legal violence of the police often rampages uncontrollably throughout the civil space, determining the law in those spaces of exception where its limits are unclear:[4]

> [T]he police intervene 'for security reasons' in countless situations where no clear legal situations exists, when they are not merely, without the slightest relation to legal ends, accompanying the citizen as a brutal encumbrance through a life regulated by ordinances, or simply supervising him. (Ibid.: 243)

We are reminded of the deployment of the ideology of 'security' to authorize exceptional police powers of detention, surveillance and violence against terrorist suspects. However, what is also evident is the mundaneness, the everydayness of police violence. The policing of protests, for instance, where police often resort to extra-legal tactics such as 'kettling', is an example of this 'exceptional' dimension of police power. So the moment of exception, the moment of the legal suspension of the law which Schmitt saw as the 'miraculous' expression of sovereign power, is not exceptional at all. As anarchists showed, it is part of the normal structure of state power and can be witnessed in everyday practices of policing. Nor is it a question of the exception being outside the law. Police violence is neither entirely inside nor entirely outside the law but, rather, inhabits a sort of no-man's land in which one blurs into the other. The law articulates itself through a violent enforcement which it cannot, at the same time, control and which exceeds its limits – a violent excess which both disturbs and constitutes the limits of the law. This continual blurring of the line, this legal ambiguity which is at the very core of police power, is why Benjamin describes it as 'formless, like its nowhere-tangible, all-pervasive, ghostly presence in the life of civilized states' (ibid.). One gets the feeling that today's societies are literally controlled by these mediocre sovereigns, especially when, more and more, we are met with the sight of heavily armed, militarized police forces on our streets prepared to use excessive violence at the slightest provocation, as we have seen recently in many cities and towns in the United States. The oppressiveness of the police is no less true in liberal-democratic states than in authoritarian states. Indeed, Benjamin makes the important point that, whereas the despotism of the police is a sort of hangover from the absolutist regimes, to whom its presence was in a way becoming, in democracies, defined by the separation of legislative and executive authority, its 'spirit' is more disturbing and devastating (ibid.).[5] In democracies, in other words, police – who claim to 'serve and protect' society – become its sovereign, inhabiting the place of power left vacant by the Prince.[6]

Moreover, if the law is to be understood through its connection to violence, at the same time violence is to be understood through its connection to law. Benjamin's critical claim is that violence is violent *through its relation to law*, whether it is the violence that preserves the legal system or violence that overthrows the legal system only to found a new one in its place. This insight makes radical politics, and questions of opposition, resistance and revolution, deeply problematic, and we are once again confronted with the ambiguity of constitutive power that I discussed in chapter 3. Benjamin's analysis would seem to confirm the suspicion that, at the heart of the constitutive power of political revolutions, there is a 'lawmaking' violence which founds a new legal-political order (constituted power) and which in turn uses violence to preserve its authority. To speak in Sorelian terms, the constitutive 'violence' of the political general strike ends up as *force* – that is, the bloody violence enacted in the name of preserving a new state order. We find in Benjamin, as we did in Sorel, an anarchistic sensitivity to the dangers of revolutionary programmes. How many revolutions in the past have violently overthrown one regime of power and law, only to establish a new one in its place? How many revolutions have only reaffirmed the place of state power, this mysterious core that unites law and violence, generating the continual oscillation between them?[7]

Divine violence

Is there a way out of this interminable circulation of violence and law which has hitherto entrapped radical politics? Is it possible to think about a form of violence which is neither lawmaking (*constitutive*) nor law-preserving (*constituted*), but which dismantles this infernal machine of sovereignty altogether? Here Benjamin introduces a further distinction between *mythic violence* and *divine violence*. Mythic violence is the violence that founds the law, which brings the law into being and fixes the subject through guilt as perpetually enthralled to it.[8] By contrast, Benjamin's enigmatic notion of 'divine violence' – violence that is not bound to the law – should be understood as a kind of anarchistic movement that strikes at the law, embodying a transformative rupture, but which at the same time does not spill blood. While mythic violence establishes and sanctifies the authority of the law, divine violence destroys the law and disrupts its boundaries. While mythic violence is on the side of power, divine violence is on the side of *justice*. Divine violence cuts the Gordian knot that binds together violence and law and, in doing so, embodies the radical dissolution and transcendence of state power: 'On the breaking of this cycle maintained by mythic forms of law, on the suspension of law with all the forces on which it depends, finally therefore on the abolition of state power, a new historical epoch is founded' (Benjamin 1996: 252–3).

It seems impossible not to read this notion of divine violence through Sorel's notion of the proletarian general strike – which Benjamin himself refers to at length, describing it as an anarchistic form of action (1996: 246). In the accounts of both Sorel and Benjamin there is an understanding of violence, not in pursuit of any particular end or programme – something which only founds a new state or new legal system – but as *pure means*: Benjamin refers to 'pure immediate violence' (ibid.: 252). Indeed, for both thinkers, what makes this radical form of violence paradoxically non-violent and bloodless is its detachment from specific ends, whether legal or otherwise. Such an understanding of action might be considered as *ontologically anarchic*.

Violence and ontological anarchy

Benjamin's divine violence – as violence against the violence of the law – releases life from the clasp of the law, saving us from this fate. He says:

> The dissolution of legal violence stems . . . from the guilt of more natural life, which consigns the living, innocent and unhappy, to a retribution that 'expiates' the guilt of mere life – and doubtless also purifies the guilty, not of guilt, however, but of law. For with mere life the rule of law over the living ceases. (1996: 250)

Yet, divine violence is more than just the destruction of the law, because this always risks, as we have seen, the establishment in its place of a new law, a new legal system. Rather, divine violence affirms life's power over law and its *indifference* to it, thus expiating and removing the law's hold over us. In this sense, it is very much like the notion of insurrection explored in chapter 3.

Divine violence is not a revolution but an insurrection,[9] and it can be likened to many examples of insurrection we have seen recently, in which the violence of the crowd seems to be without concrete strategic or political aim but often takes symbolic targets. Perhaps the violence against the ignominious spectacle of the World Cup in Brazil in 2014 might be seen as an example of divine violence, as might the insurrections in Greece against the neoliberal austerity regime and police violence, as well as the more recent uprisings against police violence in the United States.

Benjamin also points to the possibility of another conception of pure means – a world of non-violent techniques of conflict resolution which have as their basis 'courtesy, sympathy, peaceableness, trust' (1996: 244). We might think here of the non-coercive forms of communication and horizontal decision-making based on cooperation and mutual regard that characterize many radical movements today, where there is an attempt to develop forms of interaction which are autonomous from governmental practices and state institutions. The danger here is that, as Benjamin argues, these autonomous everyday forms of conflict resolution become institutionalized and legally regulated, thus taking them out of the hands of people and eliminating their spontaneity and freedom – abstracting them into relations between *objects*. They become, in Stirner's terms, 'fixed ideas' rather than real, lived relations and experiences.

Indeed, Benjamin's notion of divine violence – while it strikes from a sphere external to the human world – might be seen as the attempt to restore life to itself, to rescue it from the abstraction and alienation of the law, which always renders it guilty, and to bring it back to the realm of ordinary human experience. This is made clear in Benjamin's understanding of the judgement against violence – 'Thou shalt not kill' – not as an absolute commandment but, rather, as an ethical guideline 'for the actions of persons and communities who have to wrestle with it in solitude and, in exceptional cases, to take on themselves the responsibility of ignoring it' (1996: 250). This does not simply open the possibility of justifying real violence in certain circumstances – for self-defence, for instance – but, more importantly, proposes a notion of ethical judgement as distinct from moral commandment. In my conception of ontological anarchy, developed from Reiner Schürmann, action is no longer determined by an *a priori* moral law; it can no longer rely on such absolute foundations.[10] But this does not condemn us to nihilism; on the contrary, it opens up a sphere of autonomous ethical judgement in which one makes decisions about right or wrong in the contingency of the situation. Autonomous ethical judgement is therefore not nihilistic but *anarchistic*. And we could say that central to postanarchism is a sphere of autonomous ethical action and relationality beyond the determinations and constraints of law.

Through confronting the question of violence in the way that we have we can get a clearer sense of the ethical coordinates that ought at least to situate radical politics today. While it is too easy simply to align postanarchist politics with non-violence, I have shown how the notion of violence might be ethically transformed and sublimated into insurrectionary forms of action against institutionalized violence which do not themselves lead to the spilling of blood. At the very least, it seems to me that this 'non-violent' violence – rather than any return to Revolutionary Terror[11] – must be the ethical and political horizon of radical politics today.

5

Voluntary Inservitude

The last chapter showed how the understanding of violence in radical politics might be ethically transformed into autonomous action that transcends the paradigms of power and law – in other words, acting beyond their limits, *as if* these paradigms did not exist. The violence of postanarchism lies in its *indifference to power*, and the radical possibilities for freedom that this reveals, rather than in the blood spent in seizing it. In this chapter, I will deepen the explanation of precisely what I mean by indifference to power. And I will approach this from the opposite direction by exploring the problem – at once political and ethical – of our wilful and excessive recognition of power.

Perhaps the greatest obstacle to radical politics today – as indeed at any time – is not the formidable nature of Power but, rather, our obedience to it. As I have pointed out in an earlier chapter, contemporary liberal regimes of power operate not so much through coercion – although there is this as well – as primarily through encouraging certain forms of identification, passivity, conforming

91

behaviours, patterns of consumption and communication, and even a desire for our own domination. It is here that we encounter one of the most perplexing questions of political theory: why do people obey, even when it is not in their interests to do so? This is the old problem of voluntary servitude, diagnosed long ago by Étienne de la Boétie, who, confounded by our passivity and obedience in the face of tyrannical power, arrived at a startling conclusion: all forms of power were essentially sustained, indeed *created*, by our voluntary submission. Voluntary servitude, rather than violent coercion or even theories of ideological 'false consciousness', still serves, I would argue, as a more convincing explanation for the continuity of domination – and much of this chapter will be devoted to a contemporary exploration of La Boétie's astonishing sixteenth-century text *Discours de la servitude volontaire*. However, while the voluntary servitude hypothesis might seem on the surface to yield rather pessimistic conclusions about our continual obeisance to power, I will argue that, on the contrary, it reveals power's ultimate fragility and indeterminacy – even its *non-existence* – and therefore the radical potential for freedom.

The problem of obedience

Yet, in thinking about freedom today and its centrality to any politics of emancipation, we seem to arrive at a dead end. Not only is freedom an increasingly opaque and ambiguous concept – which is why I have suggested that 'ownness' might be a more useful category – but it is not at all clear that people actually want it. On the contrary, the most superficial glance at our contemporary world seems to reveal a desire not for freedom but for authority, for a new Master. How else does one explain the electoral success of all kinds of reactionary, authoritarian and even fascist political movements or the return of the most noxious fundamentalisms and reactionary ideologies? Is there not a clamouring for more police powers, more punitive law and order measures, tougher action against 'illegal' migrants and certain minorities, more restrictive regimes of border control, more intensive surveillance, and so on?

This would be what Deleuze and Guattari (2004) called 'micro-fascism': a kind of authoritarianism and desire for one's own repression that permeates the social body, infiltrating everyday habits, behaviours and practices, and inhabiting the politics of both the right and the left. Indeed, historical fascism itself is something which might in large part be explained by this phenomenon of voluntary servitude. In *The Mass Psychology of Fascism* (1970), by the psychoanalyst Wilhelm Reich, the explanation for the rise of National Socialism in Germany is sought not within the Marxist theory of 'false consciousness' but within the real desire on the part of the masses for their own domination, a desire that originates, Reich argues, in sexual repression. Crucially, then, the success of the Nazis was attributable not to Hitler and his supposed charisma but, rather, to the masses themselves, who in a sense created him:

> But the success of this mass organization [the NSDAP] is
> to be ascribed to the masses not to Hitler. It was man's

authoritarian freedom-fearing structure that enabled his propaganda to take root. Hence, what is important about Hitler sociologically does not issue from his personality but from the importance attached to him *by the masses*. (Reich 1970: 40; emphasis in original)

This desire for the fascist Leader arises from, as Reich puts it, an 'authoritarian freedom-fearing' structure on the part of the masses and, in particular, from the conservative attitudes and values of the lower-middle classes, which stemmed ultimately from sexual repression. These included conservative attitudes towards sexuality, a reverence for authority, an ideology of 'honour' and 'duty', and traditional patriarchal beliefs. Patriarchal authority within the family translated into the desire for an authoritarian state; the father was seen as a mini-Fuhrer, and this allowed people to identify with, and at the same time obey – according to the dynamic set out by Freud (1955) in his study of the psychology of groups – the Führer: 'Notwithstanding his vassalage, every National Socialist felt himself to be a "little Hitler"' (ibid.: 80).

No doubt psychoanalysis can tell us much about the mystery of voluntary obedience and the desire for the Master that lies within us all. There is perhaps, as Reich suggests, an authoritarian psychic structure that underlies social relations, paving the way for future fascist Masters to emerge. However, what is so perplexing about the current condition, at least in our democratic societies, is that there is no longer any visible Master to obey, and yet we obey like never before: we are, as Agamben puts it, 'the most docile and cowardly social body that has ever existed in human history' (2009: 22). Indeed, it would seem that the less visible and tangible Power is, and the less society is structured in overtly hierarchical and authoritarian ways, the more likely we are to obey. Yet who or what exactly are we obeying? Perhaps we can detect behind the abstract authority of the laws and the benign dictates of the market the hidden voice of command, which is all the more compelling for its obscurity and opacity. As I have argued, the neoliberal regimes in which we live today govern us in the name of our own freedom, and this requires our free, voluntary servitude. In other words, such regimes are conditional upon a particular form of obedience – not one generated primarily by fear or coercion but, rather, by freedom. We obey freely through our everyday patterns and rituals of behaviour and consumption – shopping, voting, communicating and enjoying in normalized ways, and even in 'abnormal' ways. It is through the continuous repetition of these habits and behaviours that power is sustained. Moreover, unlike in Reich's analysis, it is no longer necessarily the case that authoritarianism stems from conservative family values and repressive approaches to sexuality; on the contrary, it is more often than not liberal permissiveness which accompanies the increasing securitization of everyday life. We live in societies that demand both private freedom – or at least a highly commodified version thereof – and public order. Those formal freedoms and rights that we have left to us, we rarely use or use well. And, despite welcome signs of civil and digital disobedience, the prevailing attitude today seems to be one of docility. Perhaps the sadness of our times lies in the fact that – at least in formally democratic societies – there is no longer any figure of the tyrant who might otherwise serve as a cover or excuse for our cowering submission to neoliberal forms of economic and political power.

Our voluntary servitude surely poses significant problems for radical political theories, perhaps none more so than anarchism, which assumes that man naturally desires freedom yet is constrained by external and artificial bonds of power. While there was an acknowledgement among the anarchist theoreticians of the nineteenth century that human desire can indeed be perverted by power,[1] there was nevertheless a sense of optimism about the revolutionary tendencies of the masses, as indeed there was in Marxism. Anarchism above all is a philosophy of human freedom and emancipation based on an essentially optimistic view of human capacities for rational and moral action. Once power was destroyed, freedom would reign. Yet, this narrative of emancipation, like many others, encounters the central deadlock of human desire – the voluntary servitude and love of submission which thwarts these revolutionary aspirations. My point, however, is not that submission and obedience are our permanent and inevitable condition; as I shall go on to show through an exploration of La Boétie's theory, the phenomenon of voluntary servitude reveals an emancipatory dimension – an *ontological freedom* which forms the underside of all systems of power and which wants only to be discovered.

Voluntary Inservitude

La Boétie and the phenomenon of voluntary servitude

It is therefore essential that we investigate this enigmatic problem of voluntary servitude in more depth, and here I turn to the first person to diagnose this condition, the sixteenth-century figure Étienne de La Boétie. La Boétie, who was born in Sarlat in France in 1530, and who, were it not for the *Discours de la servitude volontaire* – also known as *Le Contre'un* (*Anti-One*; written probably in 1548 when he was only eighteen) – would be known only as the friend and confidant of Michel de Montaigne, asked in this essay a simple, yet scandalous question: why do men obey? It is worth quoting him at length here to get a sense of the full import of this question:

> For the present I should like merely to understand how it happens that so many men, so many villages, so many cities, so many nations, sometimes suffer under a single tyrant who has no other power than the power they give him; who is able to harm them only to the extent to which they have the willingness to bear with him; who could do them absolutely no injury unless they preferred to put up with him rather than contradict him. Surely a striking situation! Yet it is so common that one must grieve the more and wonder the less at the spectacle of a million men serving in wretchedness, their necks under the yoke, not constrained by a greater multitude than they, but simply, it would seem, delighted and charmed by the name of one man alone whose power they need not fear, for he is evidently the one person whose qualities they cannot admire because of his inhumanity and brutality toward them . . .

But O good Lord! What strange phenomenon is this? What name shall we give to it? What is the nature of this misfortune? What vice is it, or, rather, what degradation? To see an endless multitude of people not merely obeying, but driven to servility? Not ruled, but tyrannized over? ... They suffer plundering, wantonness, cruelty, not from an army, not from a barbarian horde, on account of whom they must shed their blood and sacrifice their lives, but from a single man; not from a Hercules nor from a Samson, but from a single little man. ... What monstrous vice, then, is this which does not even deserve to be called cowardice, a vice for which no term can be found vile enough, which nature herself disavows and our tongues refuse to name? (La Boétie 2008: 40–1)

We can see how this willing submission to domination, this voluntary servitude to the will of a tyrant – who is simply a creation of the abandonment of our own will and our own power – constitutes a genuine mystery for La Boétie. He is dumbfounded in the face of it and struggles to name it. It must not be confused with cowardice, he says, which, while despicable, is in some ways understandable. Here the power imbalance between the masses and the tyrant is so great that cowardice simply cannot account for the former's acquiescence to the latter; people have the power and yet they choose freely, voluntarily, to give it up to one man who lords it over them, and yet who is essentially their creation and who could be toppled without lifting a finger. How can this be explained? Like a doctor unable to diagnose his patient's condition, La Boétie struggles to identify and account for this moral sickness. There must be some sort of misdirection or aberration of the will: people, who normally, naturally, desire freedom, for some reason choose to give up this freedom and to will their own servitude.

For La Boétie, freedom is our natural condition; man is a being intended for freedom and for the enjoyment of the natural bonds of companionship and equality, not the artificial bonds of power. Servitude is so far removed from our nature that even animals resist the slightest constraint on their freedom:

> The very beasts, God help me! if men are not too deaf, cry out to them, 'Long live Liberty!' Many among them die as soon as captured: just as the fish loses life as soon as he leaves the water, so do these creatures close their eyes upon the light and have no desire to survive the loss of their natural freedom. (2008: 51)

Unlike the animals – who understand freedom better than we – we do not close our eyes but merely lower them in submission, as we become *habituated* to our own domination. To be subjected to power is therefore unnatural, and to will our own subjection to power is even more unaccountable. In this sense, La Boétie might be regarded as the anti-Hobbes. For Hobbes, the freedom that we suffer in the state of nature is unnatural to us in the sense that we cannot live in peace and security; and thus the desire to submit to absolute sovereign power – even though it is of human artifice rather than a natural form of authority – is itself absolutely natural and rational. For La Boétie, this whole rationalization of submission is reversed: we enjoy the freedom and equality, indeed, the plurality and singularity with which nature endows us; and then, for some reason, on account of some misfortune of history – which La Boétie does not or perhaps cannot explain – we give it up, and have suffered the caprices of power and the torments of servitude ever since. Pierre Clastres, in his essay on La Boétie, relates this historical misfortune to the sudden loss of primitive freedom which so-called savage man tried so hard to preserve, knowing full well the dangers of power. By suddenly entering the world of power and hierarchy – by acquiescing and thus authorizing the state-machine – primitive man does not develop but actually *regresses*; there is the fall from grace (see Clastres 2010: 171–88). Similarly, for La Boétie, people suddenly switch, quite voluntarily, from freedom to servitude. But the ontological primacy of freedom over power is the important thing here. One whole century before the shadow of Leviathan loomed up over our horizon, La Boétie had already disturbed its foundations by revealing the ontological freedom that lay beneath it, the freedom which Hobbes tried to make us forget.

Our fall into servitude has something to do with apathy; a kind of moral languor comes over us so that we no longer desire freedom and independence. But, at the same time, La Boétie is eager to stress that our servitude is *active* rather than passive. Our domination is something in which we willingly participate, the cords that bind us we renew and strengthen daily: 'you weaken yourselves in order to make him the stronger and the mightier to hold you in check' (2008: 46–7).

How does La Boétie attempt to account for what is essentially unaccountable? He proposes, tentatively, three possible factors that might explain this lamentable

Voluntary Inservitude

condition. Firstly, he says, men become accustomed to servitude such that they forget that they were ever free. Obedience and docility become a matter of habit (a 'habituation to subjection', as he puts it):

> This is why men born under the yoke and then nourished and reared in slavery are content, without further effort, to live in their native circumstance, unaware of any other state or right, and considering as quite natural the condition into which they were born . . . Let us therefore admit that all those things to which he is trained and accustomed seem natural to man and that only that is truly native to him which he receives with his primitive, untrained individuality. (2008: 54)

Secondly, La Boétie refers to the ways that power distracts us, dazzles us, seduces us with its gaudy show, with its spectacles and rituals:

> Plays, farces, spectacles, gladiators, strange beasts, medals, pictures, and other such opiates, these were for ancient peoples the bait toward slavery, the price of their liberty, the instruments of tyranny. By these practices and enticements the ancient dictators so successfully lulled their subjects under the yoke, that the stupefied peoples, fascinated by the pastimes and vain pleasures flashed before their eyes, learned subservience as naively, but not so creditably, as little children learn to read by looking at bright picture books. (Ibid.: 64)

Are we not today just as dazzled – perhaps even more so – by the magical power of the spectacle? From the banalities of celebrity culture, to the infantile excitement and almost quasi-religious fervour accompanying the launch of the latest technological gadget, to giant global entertainment and sporting events – we allow ourselves to be stupefied and made docile by spectacles of all kinds, which, in the same manner as the spectacles of the ancients, serve only the interests of power.

Thirdly, La Boétie shows how power constructs for itself a hierarchy of relations in which the tyrant's place is sustained by intricate networks and relations of dependency. Our submission and obedience are assured – bought cheaply, La Boétie would say – by pay-offs that we receive from those immediately above us. We submit to the power of another in return for our own little miserable place in the tyrant's great pyramid of power that we ourselves have constructed: 'The consequence of all this is fatal indeed. And whoever is pleased to unwind the skein will observe that not the six thousand but a hundred thousand, and even millions, cling to the tyrant by this cord to which they are tied' (2008: 72).

The impotence of power and the will to freedom

However, La Boétie's various explanations for our condition of servitude are perhaps less important than the implications of his actual diagnosis of this problem, this enigma at the heart of all political domination. But it all depends on what we take from this. If we interpret La Boétie as *simply* saying that man will always, when he gets half the chance, submit to power and cut his own throat, then the notion of voluntary servitude does not get us very far and may even give rise to a certain conservatism which says that men are born to submit. But nothing could be further, I would argue, from La

Boétie's intentions, especially when he says that freedom rather than servitude is our natural condition. Therefore, the way I propose we read his great work is in an emancipatory sense, as a call to freedom, as a way of waking us up, rousing us from our enfeebled, servile state. La Boétie does this by confronting us with a truth so astounding that it has the power, even today, to shake the foundations of political authority to their core. If we have freely chosen servitude, if we willingly participate in our own domination without the need for coercion, then this means that all power, even if it appears to bear down upon us, is essentially an *illusion*, one of our own making. If, in other words, we have created the tyrant in our act of submission to him, this means that the tyrant has no real power. The power he has over us is only *our* power in an alienated form; the chains that bind us are the chains we ourselves have forged. As La Boétie says: 'he has indeed nothing more than the power that you confer upon him to destroy you' (2008: 46).

All power is only *our* power; domination is only possible through our continuing submission, the continual offering of ourselves to power. And this realization makes power fragile and unstable. All we must do is to peer through the veils of power to see its essential weakness, its emptiness and impotence. All we must do if we want to free ourselves from the power of the tyrant, according to La Boétie, is simply to take back our power – or, even more simply, to stop giving ourselves up to him, to stop rendering our power to him, to stop this continual repetition of behaviours of submission.

So it is not even a question of overthrowing the tyrant, but simply no longer to empower him and instead to empower ourselves, upon which the tyrant will fall of his own accord and the spell of domination will be broken:

> From all these indignities, such as the very beasts of the field would not endure, you can deliver yourselves if you try, not by taking action, but merely by willing to be free. Resolve to serve no more, and you are at once freed. I do not ask that you place hands upon the tyrant to topple him over, but simply that you support him no longer; then you will behold him, like a great Colossus whose pedestal has been pulled away, fall of his own weight and break in pieces. (La Boétie 2008: 47)

The pedestal of power is one that we have erected through our continued submission; it is very easily pulled away by our refusal to submit. That all power depends on our power – this is something we have forgotten. La Boétie wants people to recall their own power or, rather, to recognize that they had the power all along, they just didn't know it. La Boétie offers us no revolutionary programmes to follow – none are needed. He simply wants us to emancipate ourselves, to emancipate ourselves from our own servitude. Crucially, we are reminded of Stirner's notion of the insurrection, which arises, as he says, out of 'men's discontent with themselves'. Releasing ourselves from this condition is a matter of the will, volition, of 'willing to be free'. La Boétie's text thus serves to remind us of our own will – how we lost it, and how we can regain it.

La Boétie's particular understanding of resistance as disobedience therefore has many parallels with the idea of insurrection I developed earlier. The insurrection – as opposed to the revolution – does not launch an assault on power but is simply an affirmation of oneself over power, whereupon power disintegrates. In other words, the existence of power is based on our acknowledgement of it – and even in some ways our opposition to it; yet, if we simply affirm ourselves, and thereby declare our indifference to power, we give ourselves the freedom to act *as though power no longer existed*. The insurrection therefore lays bare the great secret of power – its own non-existence. In other words, the fundamental lesson of both Stirner and La Boétie – as different as they are – is that *power does not exist*. To say that power is an illusion is not of course to say that it does not have real effects; rather, it is to deny *power's power* over us.

This theme of the non-existence of power is also pursued by Foucault, who analysed power relations in order to reveal their indeterminacy and historical contingency. Just as La Boétie considers the power of the tyrant an illusion, Foucault tells us that there is no such thing as Power with a capital P, that power has no essence, that it is not a substance but a relation, not a property but an intensity, and that even in the seemingly direst conditions of oppression there is always the possibility of resistance, and therefore of freedom. To see power in this way is in a sense to strip away its abstractions and to reveal the secret of freedom upon which it is founded; it is not a negation of freedom but a joyous affirmation of it.

Indeed, Foucault, whom we tend to see as a theorist of power and governmentality, was interested primarily in the question of '*how not to be governed*'. In his lecture at the Sorbonne in 1978, 'What is Critique?' (Foucault

1996), he proposes a genealogical analysis of power relations which reveals, as he puts it, their 'eventialization' (*événementialisation*) or historical contingency. In an analysis that has strange echoes of La Boétie's theory of voluntary servitude, Foucault raises the question of how and why we come to accept as normal and legitimate the hegemony of particular regimes of power/knowledge at certain historical moments. What must be investigated, in other words, is the mechanism by which we voluntarily subject ourselves to a specific mode of power – that is, the subjective threshold through which the subject binds himself to various forms of power. Importantly, the fact that a particular regime of power/knowledge/truth becomes acceptable to us does not mean that this process was inevitable or that it revealed to us some originary right that made it legitimate. On the contrary, its emergence is entirely contingent. It is as if a system of power and knowledge suddenly arises, and the violence of its imposition is at the same time indistinguishable from our free acceptance of it; these are simply two sides of the same mechanism of subjectification. But this contingent dimension of rupture, and this rejection of the notion of inevitability, means that any system of power/knowledge that emerges is always tenuous, never set in stone. They are without an essence, and as such they can always be thought otherwise and undone (ibid.: 397). This is what Foucault meant by starting his analysis of truth and power regimes from the assumption of 'non-power', as I mentioned in chapter 1.

If we take Foucault's insight here, we can see that every system of power is always fragile and haunted by the prospect of its own reversal and disappearance. So we should think of power not in terms of mastery or domination but, rather, as an unstable, impermanent set of relations and interactions. To put it quite simply, power has to be thought of as an event rather than as a transcendental reality, and, as such, it is an event that can be reversed. Thus, for Foucault, in words which directly invoke La Boétie's,

> If governmentalization is really this movement concerned with subjugating individuals in the very reality of a social practice by mechanisms of power that appeal to a truth, I will say that critique is the movement through which the subject gives itself the right to question truth concerning its power effects and to question power about its discourses of truth. *Critique will be the art of voluntary inservitude, of reflective indocility.* (1996: 386; emphasis added)

Foucault is saying, essentially, that all systems of power are not only fragile and unstable – they are, as he says, *events* without origin, essence or transcendental unity or legitimacy – but, indeed, they can emerge and become hegemonic only through our free acceptance of them. But what does this really mean? It means that freedom – the ability to think, live and act otherwise – is the ontological basis of all power. This is another way of approaching the notion of ontological anarchy, which is the thread that I have traced throughout this book. We have to be able to hear the murmur of freedom, of a yet unrealized yet always potentially realizable freedom that speaks to us incessantly through the fissures of power; we have to be attuned to its voice lest it be drowned out by power's cogs and machinery. Rather than power being the secret of freedom, as Foucault has so often been thought to say, *freedom is the secret of power*. This is obvious to anyone who chooses to listen to its insistent murmuring, to its joyous impatience. And this startling revelation – the ontological primacy of freedom, whereby every system of power/knowledge depends on our will, our acceptance – means that the undoing and reversal of this system is equally a matter of will, of decision, of free volition. Just as we will our own submission to particular forms of power, so we can will our own release from them. That is why Foucault refers to a *'decisive will to not be governed'*. Is this not an affirmation of freedom in its truest form? Not freedom as some abstract goal to be achieved or as a programme of liberation and social organization to be handed to us, but the freedom that *we always already have*.[2] The will to be free is nothing but the realization and affirmation of this ontological freedom. It is simply a matter of recalling this fact, of reminding ourselves that the power that seems to engulf us really depends on our acquiescence, our consent, and that all that is required to overturn this relationship of domination is a refusal of our servitude, a willing of our own freedom.

So there is nothing anachronistic about La Boétie's text: the classical figures of tyrants are much less important than the subjective mechanism, the strange desire that binds us to power, and this is all the more pertinent today in our contemporary regimes of neo-liberal rationality which rely on a self-subjection to its norms and codes. Of course, unlike La Boétie, Foucault would not trace voluntary servitude to one obscure but fateful historical moment, to a fall from our original state of freedom; rather, there has only ever been self-subjection in specific ways to specific regimes of power. Nevertheless, the fundamental insight is the same: that all forms of power, no matter how they are historically constituted, depend at some level on our willing acquiescence. How else could power arise? Voluntary servitude is the secret that underlies all the micro-disciplines and coercions, the institutional discourses, the regimes of surveillance, the vast 'carceral archipelago' charted by Foucault. La Boétie's text might be seen as the great key that allows us to unlock the eternal mystery of power; it shows us that power cannot exist without our own subjection to it. It sheds light on the threshold of subjectification that Foucault saw as the underside of any power relationship: why does the homosexual or madman attach himself to these institutionalized identities? Why does the factory worker allow himself to be trained so that he becomes an appendage of the machine? Why do we engage in rituals of confession that bind us to regimes of truth? Why do we, like the figure of Joseph K in Kafka's *The Trial*, so earnestly seek out our truth in the codes of power?[3] What is the hook, the clasp, the element that seduces us, that draws us in to this game of power? Yet, as I have said, the other side to this wilful docility is wilful indocility, or *voluntary inservitude* – as both La Boétie and Foucault insist.

The discipline of indiscipline

By coming to terms with the phenomenon of voluntary servitude, I hope to have revealed the ontological freedom that lies at the foundation of all systems of power, as well as forming the basis for all autonomous human thought and action. Any radical politics of emancipation today must have the audacity to affirm the non-existence of power and the ever-present possibility of freedom. It is clear, furthermore, that our release from voluntary servitude cannot be a purely individual enterprise; it must be practised associatively. However, as Stirner shows us, it cannot involve any collective determination of an ideal of freedom to be achieved, as this simply leads to new forms of domination. Yet if, as I suggest, we take the reality of freedom as our starting point rather than our end goal – the flip-side of our voluntary servitude – then we avoid this problem.

However, this does not mean that our release from voluntary servitude does not require discipline, as long as this is a discipline that we impose freely upon ourselves. It all comes back to the problem of the will: if, as La Boétie says, all that is required to release us from the enthralment to the tyrant is the will to be free, how do we generate this will? If we have become, as La Boétie says, habituated to our own domestication, such that we have forgotten what freedom means, how do we summon up the will to think and act differently? It does not necessarily come spontaneously – on the contrary, we are just as likely to spontaneously obey as to spontaneously resist. Of course, as La Boétie shows us, breaking the spell of domination is as much a matter of breaking with certain existing patterns of action and behaviour as inventing new ones; in other words, it is often a question of simply *stopping*, of no longer continuing a particular pattern of obedience. However, even this is not a completely passive gesture but, I would argue, requires a wilful and conscious expression of a different and more autonomous way of life. It seems to me, then, that the affirmation of one's freedom, or own-ness, requires forms of self-discipline – learning 'new habits of liberty' that Sorel spoke of.

As Richard Flathman argues, without discipline, there is no agency and therefore no possibility for freedom. Also, disciplinary limits must be present for freedom to be tested and measured against, agonistically (see Flathman 2003). There is the recognition that within oneself there are tendencies, desires and dependen-cies that make one more susceptible to the power of others. Thus, the forms of 'ascesis' that, for instance, are discussed by Foucault, in his later work on the ethi-cal practices of the 'care of the self' within the cultures of Greek and Roman antiquity, involve forms of self-discipline such that these tendencies can be controlled, mastered, in the interests of one's freedom. As Foucault puts it: 'the concern for the self and care of the self were required for right conduct and the proper practice of freedom, in order to know oneself . . . as well as to form oneself, to surpass oneself, to master the appetites that threaten to overwhelm one' (2000c: 285).

Moreover, such practices were *ethical* in the sense that they concerned not only oneself, but how one related to others. For the Greeks, the desire to dominate others, to exert excessive power over them, was actually an indication that one was not master of oneself; one has become intoxicated with one's own appetite for power, an appetite or desire which had taken over all others within the individual. It was a sign of weakness rather than strength. As Rousseau knew full well, if one desires to dominate others, one is much more likely to be dominated *by* others.[4] And we also find this idea reflected in Stirner's notion of ownness, which, so far from implying a crude, egoistic desire to exercise power over others, on the contrary displays an extreme sensitivity to the dangers posed to one's own autonomy by the temptations of what he calls 'possessedness' – where one becomes 'possessed' by certain passions, for power, money, sensuality, and so on, thus becoming dependent upon external objects.[5] So the lesson here from all these thinkers is that one plays the dangerous game of power only at one's own cost. La Boétie warned that those who allowed themselves to be drawn into the tyrant's great pyramid in the hope of rewards and favours, or so they can exert power over someone below them, placed themselves in great danger. So, we have here, with these practices of freedom through self-mastery and discipline, also an ethics (and I would say a politics) of non-domination.

Freedom – or ownness – as a release from our voluntary servitude is a discipline, an art – something that is learnt, that one learns from others and teaches oneself, something that is fashioned, worked on, patiently elaborated, practised at the level of the self in its relations with others. It is a work on our limits, both external and, perhaps more importantly, internal. The important point, however, is that freedom is our ever-present possibility and, indeed, our ontological condition, our point of departure. The realization and affirmation of this ontological freedom, coupled with its ethical responsibilities, might be seen as the central motif of postanarchist political theory.

6

Thinking from the Outside

Throughout this book I have sought to develop an understanding of politics based on what I have called *ontological anarchy*. My notion of postanarchism, while it takes its clear inspiration from anarchist political philosophy, at the same time differs from it in the following respect: rather than seeing anarchy – or the absence of fixed hierarchical orders – as the end goal of political action, it takes it as its starting point. What does this mean exactly? It means that political action is no longer determined by an absolute rational and moral end – by notions of the universal emancipation of mankind or the construction of the ideal society. However, insofar as anarchy, or the indeterminacy of the social order, is our ontological point of departure, it means that power and authority, because they are grounded upon their own nothingness, are always open to contestation. Therefore the horizon of political action remains open and contingent. By drawing on the thought of Stirner, Schürmann, Foucault, La Boétie and others, I have tried to show that the secret of power is its own non-existence, its own absence of foundations, and, if this is revealed and properly understood, then power loses its binding force over us. In this sense, the real implication of ontological anarchy is not nihilism, as some would suggest, but what might be called ontological freedom: *the freedom that we always already have.*

If there *is* an end goal for postanarchist political action, it is precisely the realization of this ontological freedom. Indeed, we might say that ontological freedom is both our end point *and* our starting point. The freedom that we already have thus has a paradoxical circularity, being at once the goal of, and the ontological ground for, political action. The struggle to realize our own freedom depends upon our enacting of this same freedom. We become free only when we act as though we are already free. Cause and effect, condition and goal, are the same. I will say more about this when I come to explore the question of autonomy below. But this formulation should be regarded as central to what might be termed an anarchist sensibility. To the extent that postanarchism is still a form of anarchism, it is an anarchism understood not as certain set of social arrangements, or even as a particular revolutionary project, but rather as a sensibility, a certain ethos or way of living and seeing the world which is impelled by the realization of the freedom that one already has.

In preceding chapters, I have explored different dimensions of this sensibility. I have argued that it requires a freeing of the notion of subjectivity from the fixed and essential identities which have hitherto served as the major categories of radical politics. Rather, to express the fundamental ungovernability of the subject, we need a different category – singularities – whose indeterminacy and, at least from the point of view of power, *opacity*, places their existence on a different threshold of subjectivation. The aim of radical politics is neither the recognition of different identities nor the liberation of the People or a class, but rather the affirmation of the autonomy or *ownness*, to speak in Stirner's terms, of singularities. It is with the same thematic of ontological freedom in mind that I proposed the notion of insurrection, rather than revolution, as the emerging model for radical political struggles today. While revolution seeks social transformation through political programmes, thus risking the imposition of a particular paradigm of freedom upon everyone else, the insurrection is a form of self-transformation and the assertion of one's indifference to power. Again, it is the affirmation of the freedom one already has. We find a similar idea reflected in the concept of violence against violence which I developed in chapter 4. What was important here was not only the critique of state and legal violence but also the ontologically anarchic action conveyed in the (non-violent) violence of pure means – understood in Sorel's terms as the proletarian general strike and in Benjamin's terms as divine violence. Key to both notions is a kind of non-strategic form of ethico-political action, to which self-determination and organization outside statist modes of politics are central. Lastly, the dimension of ontological freedom is conveyed in the idea of *voluntary inservitude*, which, I suggested, was the flip-side of La Boetie's problematic of voluntary servitude. If power was an illusion constructed simply out of our own voluntary obedience and self-abrogation, then all that was required for us to be free was the willingness no longer to serve power and to serve ourselves instead. Here, the freedom that one already has is implied through its own apparent negation – as the freedom one readily abandons, yet which therefore can be recalled at any moment. As I argued, though, this willing to be free requires at the same time forms of self-discipline, so that the habits of obedience can be broken and new habits of freedom can develop in their place. Obedience to oneself is the only possible alternative to obedience to others.

What emerges from ontological freedom is therefore a more affirmative politics and ethics of autonomy. If one were to ask what postanarchism wants, the only answer that can be given is *autonomy.* Autonomy is the ethico-political horizon of postanarchism. In this concluding chapter, I will therefore develop a distinctly postanarchist theory of autonomy which goes beyond the limitations of both Kantian and liberal understandings, drawing instead on poststructuralist motifs of self-making and ethical subjectivation. Furthermore, the chapter will explore the relationship between autonomy and democracy, seeing these as ultimately different and at times opposed forms of politics. Autonomy cannot be reduced to democracy – deliberative, radical, agonistic or otherwise – but proposes an entirely different ethical and political relationship.

A politics of autonomy

Autonomy can be broadly understood as self-government. Yet this has many different meanings in political theory, the most prominent of which are the Kantian notion of moral autonomy and the liberal understanding of autonomy as a sphere of individual freedom conceivable through various norms, procedures and institutions. In my view, neither offers a genuine or coherent understanding of autonomy insofar as they submit it to a certain moral idealism, thus imposing external obligations and duties upon the individual.

For Kant, as we know, autonomy is understood as rational obedience to the universal law that one wills for oneself. Kant seeks to establish an absolute rational ground for moral thinking, beyond empirical principles. Rather, morality should be based on a universal law – a categorical imperative – which can be rationally grasped. For Kant, there is only one categorical imperative which provides a foundation for all rational human action: '*Act only on that maxim whereby thou canst at the same time will that it should become a universal law*' (Kant 1963: 38). In other words, the morality of an action is determined by whether or not it should become a universal law, applicable to all situations. So, for Kant, moral law is based on freedom – the rational individual freely chooses out of a sense of duty to adhere to universal moral maxims. This autonomy of the will, then, is for Kant the supreme principle of morality. Freedom is, therefore, the ability of the individual to legislate for him- or herself, free from external forces. However, this freedom of self-legislation must be in accordance with universal moral categories. The Kantian principle of autonomy amounts to saying: *you are free to choose as long as you make the right choice, as long as you choose universal moral maxims*. Yet, for Kant, there is no contradiction here because, although adherence to moral laws is a duty and an absolute imperative, it is still a duty freely chosen by the individual. Moral laws are rationally established, and, because freedom can only be exercised by rational individuals, they will necessarily choose to obey these moral laws. In other words, an action is free only insofar as it conforms to moral and rational imperatives – otherwise it is pathological and therefore 'unfree'.

Kant's moral philosophy is a philosophy of the law. The thing that binds Kantian freedom to the law is its attachment to an absolute rationality. It is precisely because freedom must be exercised rationally that the individual finds himself dutifully obeying rationally founded universal moral laws. Yet, we find here a subjection of the individual to what Stirner would call 'fixed ideas' – moral concepts which ultimately derive their illusory universality and their coercive power from the religious categories they replaced. The law of morality thus works against genuine autonomy rather than being its guarantee: 'In the form of morality Christianity holds him prisoner, and a prisoner under *faith*' (Stirner 1995: 45). So, for Stirner, the notion of duty in the Kantian sense is irreconcilable with individual autonomy or what he calls ownness: 'Only by recognizing no *duty*, not *binding* myself nor letting myself be bound. If I have no duty, then I know no law either' (ibid.: 175).

Moreover, while, for Kant, the individual is formally 'free' to accept the moral law, he is not free to disobey the laws of the state. While there is permitted the free use of public reason to debate and deliberate over the legitimacy of laws, the citizen must nevertheless obey the sovereign. Resistance and rebellion against the state, no matter how tyrannical the actions of the government, is the worst possible crime (see Kant 1991a: 81). Indeed, for Kant, the fact that the state is founded on freedom, in the sense that it is freely contracted and exists to safeguard individual freedoms, means that our obligation must be absolute. The Kantian notion of moral autonomy acts to legitimize the power and authority of the state, not only in separating the free use of public reason from the question of our duty to the state – we can deliberate all we like but must nevertheless obey[1] – but, more particularly, in establishing the state as the ultimate expression of a universal moral and rational will to which we are bound. Put simply, because the state is a 'free' state based on rational agreement, and therefore a projection of our own autonomous will, its authority over us cannot be questioned. Moral autonomy, understood in this sense, becomes compatible with political servitude. It is illustrative to compare Kant and La Boétie here: while both believe in autonomy, the former understands it as obedience – both to the moral law and to the laws of the state – while the latter understands it as disobedience. Moreover, while Kant focuses on the free use of public reason as an expression of the rational and autonomous will, La Boétie alerts us to an under-theorized and much more enigmatic dimension of human behaviour: the free, uncoerced abandonment of one's own freedom – in other words, the willing of one's heteronomy. The path to autonomy therefore involves an individual struggle with oneself, against one's own habits and inclinations to submit – a struggle that takes place without being guided by, as Kant would have it, 'the starry heavens above me and the moral law within me' (1963: 164).

For post-Kantian liberals such as Rawls and Habermas – despite their differences – the Kantian principle of autonomy is fundamental to their conceptions of public reason and procedural justice. It is for Rawls the autonomous and rational subject who wills universalizable norms of justice; and it is for Habermas the autonomous sphere of intersubjective communication and procedures of rational deliberation and discourse ethics which can verify the conditions for a legitimate and democratic politics. Autonomy thus involves public participation in processes of deliberation in order to determine the shape of laws and institutions. However, this shift in focus from private or moral autonomy to political autonomy does not avoid the problematic assumption of a rational consensus based on universally recognized norms. And, for those who resist this rational consensus, there are disciplinary measures to enforce compliance.[2] Whether it is the universal moral law or the norms and procedures of public reason, we cannot avoid the conclusion that such claims assume an imaginary figure of the autonomous subject who must conform, or be made to conform, to such norms of behaviour and discourse. It is not simply that there is a coercive element to this liberal notion of autonomy, but that this coercion is all the more forceful insofar as obedience to these norms is seen as being in accordance with one's own autonomous rational will.

Moreover, one sees this disciplinary element at work within contemporary liberal or neoliberal polities, in which the individual is compelled to live up to an external standard of autonomy. For Stirner, the liberal citizen, as the bearer of certain rights and freedoms, had to be produced in such a way that his freedom could be expressed only in terms of his obedience to the state and its laws: 'For how could their liberalism, their "liberty within the bounds of law", come about without discipline?' (1995: 76). Today, neoliberal autonomy is defined much more narrowly in terms of economic responsibility. And what could be more tyrannical than this moral injunction to become, as Foucault would put it, the 'entrepreneur of himself' (2008: 226)? The individual is thrown back upon himself and his own resources and is forced to reduce his entire existence to a marketable and commodifiable set of behaviours and performances. Those who are judged to lack the capacities for autonomy (the unemployed, the mentally ill, the delinquent) are 'forced to be free' through the infliction of various sanctions or constraints. Liberal notions of political and economic autonomy, as different and conflicting as they are at times, still impose a duty to conform to a moral and rational ideal and thereby offer only a diminished and highly ambiguous experience of autonomy.

As I discussed in an earlier chapter, freedom and autonomy have become somewhat opaque notions today. This is largely due to the way liberal autonomy is defined in relation to an institutional regime which, in theory, safeguards certain individual rights and freedoms. Yet, precisely because the protection of these rights and freedoms depends upon the state, which at the same time determines their limits, they are entirely vulnerable and give way under the exigencies of 'security'.

Witness the aftermath of the terrorist attacks in Paris in 2015, which were widely perceived as an attack on freedom: the declarations of solidarity with the principle of *liberté* took on a strange ambiguity as they became virtually indistinguishable from official state propaganda. While the inviolability of the freedom of speech was being trumpeted everywhere, the French state was locking people up for ironic comments on social media, and Western governments were giving themselves sweeping new powers of surveillance. Liberal freedom today is absolutely hinged to the logic of security, which devours it in the name of protecting it. The danger, then, lies in seeing autonomy as a sphere of freedom delineated by institutions and laws: if we think of autonomy as something that is granted to us by the state, then it can be very easily taken out of our hands.

Voluntarism and self-constitution

It is therefore necessary, now more than ever, to develop alternative ways of thinking about autonomy which avoid the trap set by power. The neoliberal paradigm of the self-governing individual, which destroys freedom by subordinating it to the moral imperative of the market, cannot be countered by returning to the protective embrace of the 'big state'. In truth, the 'big state' never went away. Neoliberalism involves a more intensive integration of the individual into a process of state capture; it is, as Foucault showed, a rationality of government deployed through the individual and his freedom. Rather, neoliberal freedom can only be contested on its own grounds, by cultivating an alternative and more genuine experience of autonomy. This would involve different forms of subjectivation or what might be called self-making, so that the individual can unbind him- or herself from the governable identities and normalized codes of freedom that have been prescribed and constitute his or her own particular relationship with freedom. In other words, we should see autonomy not in prescriptive terms, as an idealized standard of rational freedom that one lives up to, but rather as the *freedom to be free.*

This is similar to the concerns of Richard Flathman, whom I mentioned in the preceding chapter, and whose heterodox liberalism, by his own account, converges quite closely with anarchism.[3] In contrast to disciplinary or, what Flathman calls, virtue-oriented liberalisms, which submit everything to the abstract tribunal of deliberative rationality (Kant, Habermas and Rawls), he proposes a 'wilful' or voluntarist liberalism where the emphasis is on individuality and plurality: 'Rather than Reason, its chief emblem is Will construed as largely or finally mysterious' (Flathman 1998: 13). Rather than a form of liberalism in which the autonomy of the individual is considered by the extent to which he or she conforms to rational norms of deliberation or procedural justice, Flathman's wilful liberalism, which draws upon thinkers such as Nietzsche and Montaigne, valorizes individual practices of self-enactment and self-making which may not necessarily be guided or determined by these norms. Moreover, these practices of self-enactment necessarily involve forms of self-discipline in order for the will to be cultivated.

Aside from some of the differences I have with Flathman's insistence on the need for institutionalisms, his notion of wilful liberalism bears some similarities to the form of autonomy I am proposing here. While perhaps not as radical, it has some resonance with Stirner's ethics of ownness, a concept of egoistic self-enactment that also involves forms of self-discipline in order to avoid the problem of 'possessedness' that I discussed in the previous chapter. 'Possession' undermines autonomy and presents only a one-sided and limited form of egoism, according to Stirner (1995: 70). Possessedness is a kind of obedience to a fixed idea that has taken over one's whole subjectivity. Yet we are not invoking some notion of positive freedom here, as there is no rational or moral self that one is expected to live up to. There is simply the notion of self-mastery or obedience to oneself, understood as being free from – or at least being able to resist – desires, habits and inclinations which threaten one's autonomy. As Stirner puts it: 'I am my *own* only when I am master of myself, instead of being mastered either by sensuality or by anything else (God, man, authority, law, state, church)' (ibid.: 153). We should note here that, for Stirner, whether the threat to one's autonomy is internal (sensuality) or external (institutions like law, state and church), the danger is the same: institutions can become internalized compulsions, fixed ideas, whose submission to which we come to desire; and internalized passions and desires are always in danger of materializing into external systems of domination which threaten to engulf us.

However, if we think of autonomy in this way, we are no longer really on the terrain of liberalism; already, with Flathman, it seems to me, we are at the very limits of this discourse. The forms of subjectivation or self-making that I am interested in, which are inspired by Stirner's notion of ownness, cannot be reduced to the liberal category of the individual, or at least not unproblematically so – which is why I have proposed the term 'singularities' instead. Singularity suggests a way of thinking about autonomy which is not grounded in an essential subjectivity as a fixed idea whose identity and characteristics are graspable by regimes of power, but rather as that which is grounded in an anarchic openness which leads to the destabilization of all identities. This is what Reiner Schürmann understands as ontological *an-archy* – the absence of ultimate foundations – or what Stirner takes as the nothingness at the base of one's identity, the nothingness which serves as the point of origin for egoistic self-creation: 'I, this nothing, shall put forth my *creations* from myself' (1995: 209). We should understand this in properly poststructuralist terms: the self is not an essence but a series of *becomings*, an ongoing project of self-constitution without any clear end or *telos*. From this perspective autonomy should be seen not as a state one reaches, such that one is truly and finally autonomous – for what could this be but the very end of subjectivity itself? – but, rather, as a series of agonistic practices carried out in the context of constraints and limitations, both external and internal.

This is precisely how we should read Foucault's work on the practices of subjectivation and self-constitution in ancient Greek, Roman and early Christian cultures: such practices of self-constitution, in which one's relation to oneself and to others was submitted to an intense ethical

interrogation, were practices not so much of individualization as of autonomization designed to intensify one's
capacities for self-government. What is important for
Foucault in these writings is the relationship between
the subject, truth and power. All forms of power operate through a certain regime of truth to which the
subject is bound or, more significantly, binds himself.
Truth, power and subjectivity are held together, as we
saw in the last chapter, through acts of obedience and
obligation. However, what happens when this bond of
obedience is broken? How does the disobedient subject
understand himself as one who unbinds and distances
himself not only from a certain form of power but from
certain truth acts? Foucault says: 'It is the movement of
freeing oneself from power that should serve as revealer
in the transformations of the subject and the relation
the subject maintains with the truth' (2014: 77). What
Foucault is getting at here is a certain unbinding of the
self from forms of identity that attach him to established
regimes of truth and power which make him governable:
the care of the self is in this sense precisely an *undoing* of
the self and the elaboration of different forms of subjectivation – a 'working forth of me out of the established',
as Stirner put it when describing the process of insurrection. Autonomy involves an insurrection of the self
against the fixed identities to which it is attached.

In our contemporary societies, the connection between
power, truth and subjectivity is all the more ambiguous
in the sense that the whole of life becomes fully infused
with the market, which itself is a decentred, dispersed
and spectral figure of power. If, as Foucault believed,
the market is our dominant site of veridiction today,

such that most human activities – including politics – receive their validation through its rationality alone (see Foucault 2008), then we must think about the ways by which the subject unbinds himself from this truth regime and constitutes himself in a different way. Disobedience today means more than simply transgressing certain laws – rather, the unbinding of oneself from marketized and commodified forms of existence and the invention of alternative ways of living and seeing oneself. The rupturing of the neoliberal way of life means more than simply returning to social democratic forms of redistribution – although it might involve elements of this too: it means a fundamental withdrawal of our lives from the reign of *oikonomia*.

In thinking about autonomy in these terms, it seems we are back to the ambiguous question of the will – the will to disobey, the will to break with one's existing identities and ways of living, the will to transform oneself. As I proposed in the previous chapter, Foucault, like La Boétie, is deeply concerned with the question of the will, albeit not in a psychological sense, but rather in the terms of practices of disobedience and self-constitution in response to relations of power and truth: just as at various times we voluntarily submit to certain relations of power and truth, at other times we also break with them. There could not be resistance to power if there was not the will to resist and to not be governed.[5] The dimension of the will takes on a certain intensity and brilliance if it is understood agonistically, in relation to the forms of power that threaten to limit and constrain it and which it contests. One does not need a notion of an essential, stable subject outside of power relations

– as if such a thing were possible anyway – to assert the presence of the will: the will is that which is enacted and affirmed, which illuminates the dark sky every time the subject disobeys power and acts and thinks autonomously from it.

The axiom of freedom

Following La Boétie, we could say that the will is ever present, even if it is at times misdirected: we often will our own servitude, but this means that our own freedom is equally a matter of the will. The lesson to be learnt here is that the continuity of power and domination is entirely dependent on and sustained by the continuity of this misdirected will; power has no continuity or consistency of its own – it has to be propped up and reinstituted constantly by those who submit. But this also brings with it the joyous realization that freedom is simply a matter of willing differently, of turning away from power and investing in ourselves and our own autonomy; simpler still, it is a matter of breaking with certain patterns and behaviours of obedience that sustain power. As La Boétie says, 'it is not necessary to deprive him [the tyrant] of anything, but simply to give him nothing; there is no need that the country make an effort to do anything for itself provided it does nothing against itself' (2008: 44). In this sense, the will might at times be expressed in the sense of *not acting*, or no longer acting in certain kinds of ways that reproduce submission[6] – a kind of radical 'inaction', which can be just as powerful as revolutionary action.[7]

The key insight here is that of the ever-present possibilities of freedom. This refers to what I call the *axiom of freedom*: let us try to understand freedom not as an object to be grasped, a goal to be achieved, a political project to be fulfilled or a regime to be perfected – but rather as an ontological point of departure and an axiomatic condition for human action. Once again, we *start* with freedom rather than (necessarily) finish with it; or, rather, any situation of relative freedom or unfreedom in which we find ourselves does not in any way determine our ontological freedom.[8] Possibilities for freedom always exist, and indeed freedom must be seen as the radical underside of every condition of domination. Insofar as one can be dominated, one can also be free – just as Jacques Rancière (1999) claims that the fact of inequality verifies its opposite: the axiom of equality. This is why I find Stirner's notion of ownness appealing, as the egoistic freedom which always exists regardless of external conditions. The slave is not free from the chains and blows of his master, but he nevertheless retains a sense of ownness, of self-possession, such that, at the first opportunity, he may rise up and overpower his master: 'That I then become *free* from him and his whip is only the consequence of my antecedent egoism' (Stirner 1995: 143). Here we might say there is something prior to this moment of liberation, something which makes it possible – and this is the slave's ownness and sense of himself as an autonomous being indifferent to his external constraints.

Therefore, if postanarchism is a politics of autonomy, it is a form of autonomy understood neither as a moral and rational ideal nor as an objective condition but, rather, as a certain relationship one has and cultivates with oneself based on the ever-present potentiality of freedom. It is what allows not only resistance to power but also the invention of alternative relationships and self-governing ways of life which no longer bear the imprint of the market and the state. In this sense, postanarchism does not necessarily take a specific form, nor can it be understood in terms of particular social and political institutions; rather, it should be associated with practices and experiments in living which are open-ended. The advantage in thinking about autonomy in this way is that it is not dependent on the implementation of a certain type of society or a certain set of institutions; this would be to confuse autonomy with a 'fixed idea' which risks another kind of alienation. Rather, autonomy is something that can be seen in practices and relationships that go on all around us. The task of radical political thought, it seems to me, is simply to be attuned to this anarchism of the everyday. It is therefore pointless to speculate on the contours and principles of a postanarchist society, other than to say that freedom and autonomy are possible in any situation or social arrangement, just as domination is possible in any social arrangement. Postanarchism resists its own totalization as an ideal form of society, an ideal polis; it is only interested in practices of autonomy.[9]

Autonomy and democracy

Earlier in the book, I discussed examples of contemporary political practices and forms of association that I saw as indicative of a new politics of autonomy. The mode of politics characteristic of the Occupy movements, for instance, or in horizontal activist networks suggests a form of self-organized and autonomous action which is outside the representative structures of the state. There is a conscious attempt here to create a space for new forms of political and ethical interaction, association and, indeed, subjectivation. However, my aim is not to set these examples up as a sort of prescriptive model for a radical politics. My interest is only in the potential of the practices and forms of autonomous community and subjectivity they seem to propose.

Inevitably, however, in invoking these particular forms of politics, the question of democracy arises. Contemporary movements such as Occupy offer many examples of democratic innovation modelled on participatory democracy. Indeed, many have looked to Occupy and other contemporary movements as providing an answer to the democratic deficit of our times by providing a directly democratic forum – with popular assemblies evoking the idea of the Athenian agora – where all voices can be heard and all opinions and perspectives addressed. I do not of course disagree with this: the democratic innovativeness of Occupy was one of its most striking and important features, and it offered an infinitely more desirable and legitimate model of democratic politics than our decrepit and oligarchic representative processes. We were given a glimpse, for the first time in many years, of what a real participatory democracy could look like, in stark contrast to the insufferable inequality and tyranny of our formal liberal-democratic institutions. Indeed, it is quite possible that these recent democratic movements and convergences have unleashed something like a worldwide democratic revolution, with the rise to prominence of radical political parties such as Podemos and Syriza, which have either emerged from or been galvanized by these alternative democratic forums. Instances of convergence between some radical movements and left-wing anti-austerity political parties are perhaps the start of a different kind of democratic experiment, which, at this time and when compared with the official alternatives on offer, can only be welcomed.

However, autonomous and postanarchist politics today is not, in my view, reducible to democracy – and if we look only to the democratic mechanisms of contemporary movements, then we are missing what is vital about them. Indeed, rather than seeing new forms of decentralized activism – and here I have spoken not only of Occupy but also of marginal networks of resistance such as Anonymous – entirely in terms of their democratic quality, I prefer to see them as forms of singularization and voluntary inservitude. Just as impressive as their meticulous democratic procedures is their gesture of disobedience and defiance in the face of power – or, rather, the way that, along the lines of Stirner's insurrection, those who participate in these forms of politics discover and enact their ontological freedom, acting as though power no longer existed. In other words, there is an expression here of a kind of self-affirmation, at once collective and highly individualistic; we might call it a politics of ownness, in which the sovereignty of singular wills and desires, intensified through interaction with others, affirmed its sheer indifference to power. We might think of it as a demonstration of power's non-existence. Just as the Cynics, those original anarchists, defiled and disrupted the Athenian agora through their parrhesiastic life,[10] and just as Sorel's proletarians affirmed themselves in their freedom and joyous egoism by occupying the means of production, singularities today carve out an autonomous plane of life and experience. We must think of the movements of Occupation and resistance today, aside from their democratic potential, as precisely a staging of this autonomous life.

It is necessary, then, to reflect on the relationship between autonomy and democracy. Perhaps we can say that democracy is a necessary, yet not sufficient, condition for autonomy. Like Cornelius Castoriadis (1991), I recognize a connection between direct democracy, as a form of self-instituting society, and political autonomy. However, I would also argue that democratic politics, in whatever form, does not in any sense exhaust our understanding of autonomy and should be seen as only one possible matrix of autonomous politics and ethics. As anarchists have always recognized, democracy, even of the direct kind, can pose a threat to the autonomy of the individual.[11] Insofar as democracy is a form of popular sovereignty, it implies a subordination of the individual not simply to the majority will but to an abstract and alienating fixed idea, a spectral collectivity which stands outside the power of the individual. If it is a direct democracy, it still constitutes itself as a totalizing regime of power – a form of state – which subordinates the self-will of the individual to an alien will. As Stirner puts it: 'We are accustomed to classify states according to the different ways in which "the supreme might" is distributed. If an individual has it – monarchy; if all have it – democracy; etc. Supreme might then! Might against whom? Against the individual and his self-will' (1995: 176). The democratic will of all does not necessarily guarantee the autonomy of the individual and, indeed, may easily work against it. Democratic sovereignty and autonomy are therefore two very different principles: the first is collectivist and absorbs the individual into a spectral body of the People, which tends to be a figure of state sovereignty; the second is singular and embodies the possibility of ethical and political difference which may at times go against the will of the People. Nietzsche might regard this as an aristocratic principle which resists the slave morality of democratic egalitarianism. I prefer to think of this – following Stirner, and to avoid any sort of Nietzschean nostalgia for aristocratic culture – as an 'egoistic' principle which is available to all and is not necessarily incompatible with democratic equality, but which nevertheless opens up a different horizon: that of ethical and political self-transformation. This idea of autonomy as ethical differentiation is also how we might understand Sorel's insistence that proletarians radically distinguish themselves from bourgeois values and modes of politics and develop their own aristocratic values of heroism and asceticism. In this sense, anarchism has often been described as an *aristocracy of all*, rather than a democracy.

As with the principle of aristocratic values, there is a clear *agonistic* dimension to postanarchist politics – an ethical contestation of external relations of domination, and also within oneself and against one's own tendencies

to submit. Ethical self-discipline and practices of ownness are the key themes here. However, we should be
clear that this ethical agonism has little to do with the
notion of agonistic democracy, at least as elaborated by
those such as Chantal Mouffe. While, for Mouffe, the
conflictual dimension is central to her understanding
of politics – in opposition to deliberative and liberal
conceptions in which the achievement of a consensus
through following certain procedures and adhering to
rational norms is the presupposed outcome – and while
she asserts, as I do, the contingency of the social order
as her ontological starting point, she nevertheless draws
from this very different political conclusions: that the
only possible principle of politics is the sovereign state,
and the only possible means of expression is representation and the hegemonic construction of a project of
power (see Mouffe 2013). Yet this conception of agonistic politics neglects, I think, a much more fundamental
form of agonism – between autonomous movements
and practices, on the one hand, and the principle of state
sovereignty itself, on the other. As I have suggested,
practices of self-organization, while they might be
flawed and problematic, have to be seen as attempts to
construct an autonomous space of political life, which,
in itself, is already a declaration of war against the current order. To dismiss such gestures and practices as
non-political, as Mouffe does, is to refuse to see their
genuinely agonistic dimension. So, postanarchism, as
a form of agonistic anarchism, resituates the dimension of 'the political' from the ontological order of the
state, in which the political is regulated and policed (in
which politics becomes synonymous with power), to the

dissenting world of contemporary practices and movements which seek autonomy from this order. Agonism for me is inextricable from the idea of autonomy. But here we should reverse the understanding of the 'autonomy of the political' put forward by Mouffe and others, for whom the specificity of politics always refers to struggles over sovereign state power. Rather, I would say that, if it means anything today, the autonomy of the political means the politics of autonomy.

The central challenge for radical politics today is not to develop better procedures and channels for democratic deliberation; it is not to make a fetish of democracy. Rather it is to think the collective with and through the individual, to think of forms of association and community which at the same time do not eclipse singular projects of ownness and ethical self-transformation but which, on the contrary, are intensified by these differences. As I suggested in chapter 2, Stirner's paradoxical notion of the 'union of egoists' might provide some answers here, or at least open up this question as the impossible yet necessary horizon of radical politics. What seems to me genuinely innovative about many contemporary movements – and here once again Occupy is exemplary – are the open and rhizomatic forms of association they offer, which are of a very different kind to formal state institutions, as well as from political parties and traditional labour organizations. Those are the models of association of the past. Because contemporary rhizomatic associations are not invested in the project of seeking power or communicating interests through the usual democratic channels, because they are concerned more with fostering autonomous relations and practices between singularities, they have an entirely different structure. This is why I do not think it is appropriate to apply the Gramscian model of hegemonic politics here.[12] Rather than attempting to construct a People to take control of state power – a project which can be achieved only through representatives who end up alienating 'the People' from its own power – radical politics today affirms a sovereign indifference to power.

The postanarchist horizon

What does it mean to be indifferent to power? It does not mean to ignore power's effects but, rather, to recognize that power itself has no consistency or substance, that it is a hollow entity, a 'spook' in Stirner's words, and that its hold over us is illusory. It means that there is nothing to grasp and nothing to fear, and that the project of seizing power is as much a form of self-abandonment as one's submission to it. It is to recognize that Power is created by us, and that it can just as easily be uncreated by us. It is to act as if power no longer existed and to live in a world that is no longer determined by its ontological principle. Postanarchism, simply put, is a form of politics and ethics based on an indifference to Power.

The wager of this book is that the tectonic plates of our age are shifting, that familiar and once hegemonic institutions and principles – both economic and political – appear increasingly empty and lifeless to us, that the great secret of Power's non-existence is being revealed.

Whether this can be explained as the epochal closure of metaphysics, as Heideggerians would have it, or as the end of the metanarrative, as postmodernists would maintain, it cannot be understood apart from the redis- covery of the will and affirmation of the possibilities of autonomous life. Of course, this moment has many dangers, not least of all the desire to restore the princi- ple of authority, to fill in its empty place with new and terrifying proliferations of power. No radical political project can assure itself that it is safe from this eternal temptation. At the same time, the ontologically anarchic condition, which is increasingly revealing itself to us, presents us with an open horizon for creative political thought and action. The task of radical politics today is not to establish a new hegemony over this empty horizon but, rather, to cultivate and affirm the forms of life and the practices of freedom which already render it visible.

Notes

Chapter 1 From Anarchism to Postanarchism

1 Nor does it lead, as Schürmann maintains, to totalitarianism or the 'anarchy of power' but, rather, to the withering of the very principle of Power (see Schürmann 1987: 290–1).

2 Indeed, Salvo Vaccaro suggests that anarchism should not see itself as a philosophy based on stable ontological foundations; this static order of truth mirrors the sovereign principle of the state. Rather than grounding itself in an *arché*, anarchism, insofar as it is inseparable from real historical *movements*, should embrace a more pluralistic and dynamic ontology of becoming (see Vaccaro 2013). A similar point is made by Hakim Bey (1991), whose concept of *ontological anarchy* emphasizes Chaos and movement as the law of all existence.

3 In an interview, Foucault said: 'this practice of liberation is not in itself sufficient to define the practices of freedom that will still be needed if this

people, this society, and these individuals are able to define admissible and acceptable forms of existence or political society' (2000c: 282–3).

Chapter 2 Singularities

1 I am referring here to forms of right-wing, free-market libertarianism rather than to anarchism.
2 A reference to Foucault's formula for biopower: 'a power to *foster* life or to *disallow* it to the point of death' (1981: 138; emphasis in original).
3 I am referring to Hardt and Negri's (2001) thesis of the multitude.
4 The black bloc tactic originated with the German Autonomen movement in the 1970s and 1980s.
5 I rely on the Steven Byington translation (see Stirner 1995).
6 All emphasis for quotations from Stirner appears in the original.

Chapter 3 Insurrection

1 It is significant that Stéphane Hessel, in his essay *Time for Outrage!* (*Indignez-vous!*) (2011), which was the inspiration for radical mobilizations such as the Indignados in Spain and the Occupy movement, speaks of *insurrection* rather than revolution.
2 This idea is also explored by Franco Berardi (2012: 133), who sees the insurrection, or what he calls the Uprising, as a form of therapy for some of

the psychopathologies engendered by late modern capitalism.

3 In this sense, this form of action is not incompatible with the notion of invisibility and anonymity that I developed in the previous chapter.

4 Indeed, Arendt was critical of the French Revolution precisely because, in her eyes, it brought questions of survival and necessity onto the political stage – thus presenting a contamination of the properly political realm with matters of bare life (see Arendt 2009).

5 See my and John Lechte's critique of the Arendtian conception of civic life (Lechte and Newman 2013).

6 The Cynic life was, according to Foucault, an unalloyed, sovereign life which was autonomous from others: 'a life without bonds, without dependence on anything that might be foreign to it' (2011: 255).

7 For an overview of the 'sustainable de-growth' paradigm, see Martínez-Alier et al. (2010). In speaking of de-growth as an autonomous way of life, I am also inspired by Jacques Ellul's critique of technological civilization (see Ellul 1965), as well as Ivan Illich's (1985) emphasis on 'conviviality' – as opposed to industrial productivity – in reference to autonomous practices, skills, and forms of self-sufficiency in fields of healthcare, education, transportation, housing and agriculture.

8 This understanding of insurrection, as distinct from revolution, is also reflected in Howard Caygill's discussion of resistance: 'As a political model insurrection also evokes the gesture of defiance, but emphasizing a sustained uprising rather than the

instrumental, goal-oriented activity of revolution' (2013: 199).

Chapter 4 Violence against Violence

1 It should by now be clear that I do not include within this category acts of 'violence' against property, which in certain instances – e.g., the vandalism and destruction of corporate and state-military property – can be seen as being entirely legitimate.

2 With Sorel's insistence on the need of workers to affirm their 'egoism' – or, in Marxian terms, for the workers to become a class 'for itself' – we are also reminded of Stirner's philosophy of egoism, which, as I have suggested, is one not of simple selfishness but, rather, of individual uniqueness and autonomy.

3 It is surprising that, in many of the readings of Benjamin's text, the influence of Sorel tends to be underplayed.

4 As I write these words, juries in the US have decided not to indict the police officers involved in the killing of unarmed citizens in Ferguson, Missouri, and New York City – a clear case, it would seem, of legal murder.

5 The recent stand-off between the NYPD and the mayor of New York is an interesting case of a dispute between civil and legal authority (the state) and its violent excrescence (the police), which is not always subject to the former's control.

6 A reference to Claude Lefort's thesis about

democratic regimes being characterized by a symbolically empty place of power (see Lefort 1988).

7 It is worth bearing in mind that the German word *Gewalt* in the title ('Kritik der Gewalt') means not only violence but also power and force.

8 Benjamin's example is the mythical figure Niobe, whose children are slaughtered by the gods as punishment for her hubris, and who is transformed into a petrified stone waterfall whose incessant weeping is a constant testament to her transgression. Benjamin's point here is that the law is our fate, and it is only through the radical intercession of what he calls divine violence that we have any hope of escaping it.

9 Benjamin does associate divine violence with the possibilities of 'revolutionary violence' – but I think *insurrection* is a more appropriate term for the form of action which this singular understanding of violence suggests.

10 For Schürmann, the anarchy principle, according to which action or praxis takes place without a 'why', without a *telos*, does not produce nihilism but rather 'thoughtfulness' and even leads to a new understanding of ethical 'responsibility'. Furthermore, as Schürmann shows, the anarchy principle, as it operates in Heidegger's thought, works to displace forms of institutionalized violence, particularly that which is embodied in technology: 'The violence Heidegger espouses before the institutionalized assault is the non-violence of thinking. Indeed, what is thinking's "non-violent" power? It is to do what presencing does: to let be' (Schürmann 1987:

277). This letting be marks the passage from violence to anarchy.

11 Here I make reference to a certain fetishization of political violence in thinkers such as Alain Badiou and Slavoj Žižek, who seem to regard revolutionary terror as a sign of political authenticity. The violent legal proscriptions of the Jacobin Terror of 1793–4, the state terror implemented by the Bolsheviks and the excessive violence of the Cultural Revolution, with its noxious cults of personality, are held up by these two militant philosophers as examples of genuine political events, in comparison with which the radical political mobilizations of today are largely dismissed as insignificant and trivial. See for example Badiou's discussion on revolutionary terror as an expression of the egalitarian maxim (2009: 25–7). In the same vein, Žižek indulges in a curious misreading of Benjamin's notion of divine violence, associating it with Robespierre and the Jacobin Terror – in other words, with precisely the form of state-legal violence that divine violence opposes (see Žižek 2008).

Chapter 5 Voluntary Inservitude

1 For Bakunin, the danger in Marxist and socialist political programmes which sought to capture and command state power lay in their neglect of the way that the temptations of power would corrupt even the most idealistic and committed revolutionaries: 'We of course are all sincere socialists and

revolutionists and still, were we to be endowed with power . . . we would not be where we are now' (1953: 249).

2 As Foucault put it in an interview: 'My role . . . is to show people they are much freer than they feel' (see Foucault 1988: 9–15).

3 Kafka's *The Trial* might be understood in part as a mediation on voluntary servitude: rather than escaping the clasp of the law, which does not forcibly entrap him – on the contrary, it tries to repel and elude him – Joseph K persistently seeks his place within it, and in doing so constitutes the law's domination over him. We also recall here Kafka's parable of the man from the countryside who waits and waits for the Door of the Law to admit him, only to have it shut in his face.

4 Jean-Jacques Rousseau (1987): 'It is very difficult to reduce to obedience someone who does not seek to command.'

5 Stirner actually equates possessedness with obedience (see Stirner 1995: 80).

Chapter 6 *Thinking from the Outside*

1 This distinction between the free and autonomous use of public reason in matters of conscience, and the obligation nonetheless to obey the laws and commands of the sovereign, is central to Kant's understanding of enlightenment (see Kant 1991b).

2 Rawls makes reference to punishments and penalties to enforce compliance with his 'institutions of

justice' (1999: 504). We should also note his reservations over civil disobedience and the problems posed by consent for his understanding of obligation (ibid.: 308–12).

3 Flathman (1998) calls himself a 'would-be anarchist', by which he means that, while he shares anarchism's critique of political authority, he nevertheless retains a liberal's scepticism about the claim that people can live without state institutions.

4 Schürmann (1986) associates Foucault's work with a project of 'anarchistic self-constitution': the anarchist subject, as opposed to the merely transgressive subject who seeks only to defy the law and thereby reaffirm it, resists instead the principle of social totalization enshrined in the modern state and develops for himself his own path of life and action.

5 Foucault, in an interview about the Iranian revolution, emphasized the importance of the will in the analysis of power and resistance to it, as well as in the self-constitution of the subject: 'It seems to me that we cannot do an effective analysis of power relations without introducing the issue of the will . . . The will, I would say, is what, beyond any calculation and interest, and even beyond immediate desires, can say "I prefer my death". And this is the death trial . . . The will does not need to be irrational nor to empty the subject of its desires. If you want, we can say that the will is what fixes the subject to its own position. The will is the pure act of the subject. And the subject is what is fixed and determined by this will' (see Foucault and Sassine 1979).

6 Indeed, it is astonishing the way that Power today

constantly elicits our engagement and communication – from continual polling and focus groups to the pervasive use of social media networks for political communication and commercial marketing. One detects a sense of desperation in all of this, as Power, which depends for its nourishment on endless loops of feedback and 'opinion', confronts an increasingly mute and indifferent audience – a hopeful sign, perhaps, that people are starting to turn their backs on this game of recognition.

7 Giorgio Agamben hints at something very similar with his notion of *inoperativity*, which points to the possibility of a mode of life without function or vocation, a way of living freed from the category of 'usefulness' (in my terms, an ontologically anarchic life), something which – once wrested from power and reclaimed for politics – deactivates the machine of *oikonomia* (see Agamben 2011: 166, 250–1). See also Agamben's work on St Paul, in which he proposes Stirner's notion of *insurrection* as one possible articulation – the 'ethical-anarchic' one – of the Pauline *as not*, understood here as a refusal of vocation or, to be more precise, a rendering inoperative of all vocations and juridical–factical identities (Agamben 2005: 23).

8 This is why Jean-Luc Nancy insists that freedom cannot be 'a question'; moreover, 'thinking freedom requires thinking not an idea but a singular fact' (1993: 165).

9 So far I have not drawn much in this discussion on theories of Autonomous Marxism and Autonomia. This is not to neglect the importance of these

traditions and movements on contemporary forms of radical politics – especially with regard to direct action and a refusal of hierarchical and representative forms of politics – or their many points of convergence with anarchism and poststructuralism. My aim, however, has been to develop a slightly different approach to autonomous politics, one that is grounded not in notions of class power and its relation to the dynamics of the capitalist system but, rather, on the philosophical conception of ontological anarchy.

10 As Foucault says about the Cynic philosopher, the theme of the sovereign life is turned into 'the life of battle and struggle against and for the self, against and for others' (2011: 283). Also Maurizio Lazzarato (2014) develops Foucault's argument that the question of ethical differentiation and subjectivation posed by Cynic parrhesia cut across the principle of democratic equality.

11 Robert Paul Wolff (1970: 71) argues that the conclusion of philosophical anarchism is that autonomy – which he nevertheless understands in a Kantian moral sense – is ultimately irreconcilable with virtually all forms of government, and that democratic governments command no greater sense of obligation and legitimacy than other kinds.

12 I am referring mostly to the radical democratic theories of Laclau and Mouffe, for whom the hegemonic project of building alliances between different identities and interests in order to fill the symbolically empty place of power is the central task of democratic politics (see Laclau and Mouffe 1985).

References

Agamben, G. (1993) *The Coming Community*, trans. M. Hardt. Minneapolis: University of Minnesota Press.

Agamben, G. (1998) *Homo sacer: Sovereign Power and Bare Life*, trans. D. Heller-Roazen. Stanford, CA: Stanford University Press.

Agamben, G. (2000) *Means without End: Notes on Politics*, trans. V. Binetti and C. Casarino. Minneapolis: University of Minnesota Press.

Agamben, G. (2005) *The Time that Remains: A Commentary on the Letter to the Romans*, trans. P. Dailey. Stanford, CA: Stanford University Press.

Agamben, G. (2009) *What is an Apparatus?*, trans. D. Kishik and S. Pedatella. Stanford, CA: Stanford University Press.

Agamben, G. (2011) *The Kingdom and the Glory: For a Theological Genealogy of Economy and Government* (*Homo sacer* II, 2), trans. L. Chiesa. Stanford, CA: Stanford University Press.

Arendt, H. (1999) *The Human Condition*. Chicago: University of Chicago Press.

References

Arendt, H. (2009) *On Revolution*. Rev. edn, London: Penguin.

Badiou, A. (2009) *Logics of Worlds: Being and Event*, 2, trans. Alberto Toscano. London: Continuum.

Bakunin, M. (1950) *Marxism, Freedom and the State*, trans. K. J. Kenafick. London: Freedom Press.

Bakunin, M. (1953) *Political Philosophy of Mikhail Bakunin: Scientific Anarchism*, ed. G. P. Maximoff. London: Free Press of Glencoe.

Benjamin, W. ([1921] 1996) 'Critique of Violence', in *Walter Benjamin 1913–1926*, Vol. 1: *Selected Writings*, ed. M. Bullock and M. W. Jennings. Cambridge, MA: Belknap Press, pp. 236–52.

Berardi, F. (2009) *The Soul at Work: From Alienation to Autonomy*. Los Angeles: Semiotext(e).

Berardi, F. (2012) *The Uprising: On Poetry and Finance*. Los Angeles: Semiotext(e).

Bey, H. (1991) *T.A.Z.: The Temporary Autonomous Zone, Ontological Anarchy, Poetic Terrorism*. Brooklyn, NY: Autonomedia.

Bonanno, A. (1988) *From Riot to Insurrection: Analysis for an Anarchist Perspective against Post-Industrial Capitalism*, http://theanarchistlibrary.org/library/alfr edo-m-bonanno-from-riot-to-insurrection-analysis-for-an-anarchist-perspective-against-post.

Bookchin, M. (1982) *The Ecology of Freedom: The Emergence and Dissolution of Hierarchy*. Palo Alto, CA: Cheshire Books.

Brown, W. (1995) *States of Injury: Power and Freedom in Late Modernity*. Princeton, NJ: Princeton University Press.

Castoriadis, C. (1991) *Philosophy, Politics, Autonomy:*

Essays in Political Philosophy, trans. and ed. D. A. Curtis. Oxford: Oxford University Press.

Caygill, H. (2013) *On Resistance: A Philosophy of Defiance*. London: Bloomsbury.

Clastres, P. (2010) *Archaeology of Violence*, Cambridge, MA: MIT Press.

Dean, J. (2010) *Blog Theory: Feedback and Capture in the Circuits of the Drive*. Cambridge: Polity.

Dean, J. (2012) *The Communist Horizon*. London: Verso.

Deleuze, G. (1992) 'Postscript on the Societies of Control', *October*, 59 (winter): 3–7.

Deleuze, G., and Guattari, F. (2004) *A Thousand Plateaus: Capitalism and Schizophrenia*, trans. B. Massumi. London: Continuum.

Deleuze, G., and Negri, A. (1995) 'Control and Becoming', in G. Deleuze, *Negotiations*. New York: Columbia University Press, pp. 169–76.

Ellul, J. (1965) *The Technological Society*, trans. J. Wilkinson. London: Jonathan Cape.

Flathman, R. E. (1998) *Reflections of a Would-Be Anarchist: Ideals and Institutions of Liberalism*. Minneapolis: University of Minnesota Press.

Flathman, R. E. (2003) *Freedom and its Conditions: Discipline, Autonomy, and Resistance*. New York: Routledge.

Foucault, M. (1981) *The Will to Knowledge: The History of Sexuality*, Vol. 1, trans. R. Hurley. London: Penguin.

Foucault, M. (1988) 'Truth, Power, Self: An Interview with Michel Foucault' (October 25), in *Technologies of the Self: A Seminar with Foucault*, ed. L. H.

Martin, H. Gutman and P. H. Hutton. London: Tavistock, pp. 9–15.

Foucault, M. (1991) *Discipline and Punish: The Birth of the Prison*, trans. A. Sheridan. London: Penguin.

Foucault, M. (1996) 'What is Critique?', trans. K. P. Geiman, in *What is Enlightenment? Eighteenth-Century Answers and Twentieth-Century Questions*, ed. J. Schmidt. Berkeley: University of California Press, pp. 382–98.

Foucault, M. (2000a) '*Omnes et singulatim*: Toward a Critique of Political Reason', in *Power: Essential Works of Foucault 1954–1984*, ed. J. Faubion, trans. R. Hurley et al. London: Penguin, pp. 298–325.

Foucault, M. (2000b) 'The Subject and Power', in *Power: Essential Works of Foucault 1954–1984*, ed. J. Faubion, trans. R. Hurley et al. London: Penguin, pp. 326–48.

Foucault, M. (2000c) 'The Ethics of the Concern for the Self as a Practice of Freedom', in *Ethics: Essential Works of Foucault 1954–1984*, Vol. 1, ed. P. Rabinow, trans. R. Hurley et al. London: Penguin, pp. 281–302.

Foucault, M. (2008) *The Birth of Biopolitics: Lectures at the Collège de France 1978–1979*, ed. M. Senellart, trans. G. Burchell. Basingstoke: Palgrave Macmillan.

Foucault, M. (2011) *The Courage of Truth (The Government of Self and Others II): Lectures at the Collège de France, 1983–1984*, trans. G. Burchell. Basingstoke: Palgrave Macmillan.

Foucault, M. (2014) *On the Government of the Living: Lectures at the Collège de France 1979–80*, ed. M.

Senellart, trans. G. Burchell. Basingstoke: Palgrave Macmillan.

Foucault, M., and Sassine, F. (1979) 'Entretien inédit avec Michel Foucault', http://fares-sassine.blogspot. fr/2014/08/entretien-inedit-avec-michel-foucault. html.

Freud, S. (1955) 'Group Psychology and the Analysis of the Ego', *The Standard Edition of the Complete Psychological Works of Sigmund Freud*, trans. J. Strachey, Vol. XVIII: *1920–1922*, London: Hogarth Press, pp. 67–143.

Godwin, W. (1968) *Anarchist Writings*, ed. P. Marshall. London: Freedom Press.

Graeber, D. (2002) 'The New Anarchists', *New Left Review* 13 (Jan–Feb): 61–73.

Graeber, D. (2004) *Fragments of an Anarchist Anthropology*. Chicago: Prickly Paradigm Press.

Hardt, M., and Negri, A. (2001) *Empire*. Cambridge, MA: Harvard University Press.

Hessel, S. (2011) *Time for Outrage!*, trans. D. Searls with A. Arrikha. London: Quartet Books.

Illich, I. (1985) *Tools for Conviviality*. London: Boyars.

Invisible Committee (2009) *The Coming Insurrection*. Los Angeles: Semiotext(e).

Kant, I. (1963) *Critique of Practical Reason*, trans. T. K. Abbot. London: Longmans.

Kant, I. (1991a) 'Theory and Practice: Part II', in *Political Writings*, ed. H. Reiss. Cambridge: Cambridge University Press, pp. 73–87.

Kant, I. (1991b) 'What is Enlightenment?', in *Political Writings*, ed. H. Reiss. Cambridge: Cambridge University Press, pp. 54–60.

References

Kropotkin, P. (1972) *Mutual Aid: A Factor of Evolution*, ed. P. Avrich. New York: New York University Press.

Kropotkin, P. (1987) *The State: Its Historic Role*. London: Freedom Press.

La Boétie, E. de (2008) *The Politics of Obedience: The Discourse of Voluntary Servitude*, trans. H. Kurz, ed. M. Rothbard. Auburn, AL: Ludwig von Mises Institute.

Laclau, E. (2005) *On Populist Reason*. London: Verso.

Laclau, E., and Mouffe, C. (1985) *Hegemony and Socialist Strategy: Towards a Radical Democratic Politics*, trans. W. Moore and P. Cammack. London: Verso.

Landauer, G. (2010) 'Weak State, Weaker People', *Revolution and Other Writings: A Political Reader*, ed. and trans. G. Kuhn. Oakland, CA: PM Press, pp. 213–14.

Lazzarato, M. (2014) *Signs and Machines: Capitalism and the Production of Subjectivity*, trans. J. D. Jordan. Los Angeles: Semiotext(e).

Lechte, J., and Newman, S. (2013) *Agamben and the Politics of Human Rights: Statelessness, Images, Violence*. Edinburgh: Edinburgh University Press.

Lefort, C. (1988) *Democracy and Political Theory*. Cambridge: Polity.

Lyotard, J.-F. (1991) *The Postmodern Condition: A Report on Knowledge*, trans. G. Bennington and B. Massumi. Manchester: Manchester University Press.

Martínez-Alier, J., Pascual, U., Vivien, F.-D., and Zaccai, E. (2010) 'Sustainable De-growth: Mapping the Context, Criticisms and Future Prospects of an Emergent Paradigm', *Ecological Economics* 69: 1741–7.

Mouffe, C. (2013) *Agonistics: Thinking the World Politically.* London: Verso.

Nancy, J.-L. (1991) *The Inoperative Community*, ed. and trans. P. Connor et al. Minneapolis: University of Minnesota Press.

Nancy, J.-L. (1993) *The Experience of Freedom*, trans. B. McDonald. Stanford, CA: Stanford University Press.

Nancy, J.-L. (2000) 'Being Singular Plural', in *Being Singular Plural*, trans. R. D. Richardson and A. E. O'Byrne. Stanford, CA: Stanford University Press.

Negri, A. (1999) *Insurgencies: Constituent Power and the Modern State*, trans. M. Boscagli. Minneapolis: University of Minnesota Press.

Newman, S. (2001) *From Bakunin to Lacan: Anti-Authoritarianism and the Dislocation of Power.* Lanham, MD: Lexington Books.

Newman, S. (2011) *Max Stirner.* Basingstoke: Palgrave Macmillan.

Rancière, J. (1999) *Disagreement: Politics and Philosophy*, trans. J. Rose. Minneapolis: University of Minnesota Press.

Rawls, J. (1999) *A Theory of Justice.* Rev. edn, Cambridge, MA: Harvard University Press.

Reich, W. (1970) *The Mass Psychology of Fascism*, ed. M. Higgins and C. M. Raphael. New York: Farrar.

Rousseau, J.-J. (1987) 'Discourse on the Origin of Inequality', in *Basic Political Writings*, trans. D. A. Cress. Indianapolis: Hackett, pp. 25–81.

References

Schmitt, C. (1996) *The Concept of the Political*, trans. G. Schwab. Chicago: University of Chicago Press.

Schürmann, R. (1986) 'On Constituting Oneself an Anarchist Subject', *Praxis International* 6(3): 294–310.

Schürmann, R. (1987) *Heidegger on Being and Acting: From Principles to Anarchy*, trans. C.-M. Gros. Bloomington: Indiana University Press.

Sorel, G. ([1908] 1961) *Reflections on Violence*, trans. T. E Hulme and J. Roth. New York: Collier Books.

Stirner, M. (1995) *The Ego and its Own*, ed. David Leopold, trans. S. Byington. Cambridge: Cambridge University Press.

Vaccaro, S. (2013) 'Critique of Static Ontology and Becoming Anarchy', trans. J. Cohn, *Anarchist Developments in Cultural Studies* 2: 121–37.

Wolff, R. P. (1970) *In Defense of Anarchism*. Berkeley: University of California Press.

Žižek, S. (2008) *Violence: Six Sideways Reflections*. New York: Picador.

Index

157

Index

Index

Index